TWELVE STEPS
TO A
COMPASSIONATE LIFE

TWELVE STEPS
TO A
COMPASSIONATE LIFE

Karen Armstrong

ALFRED A. KNOPF · NEW YORK · TORONTO · 2011

THIS IS A BORZOI BOOK
PUBLISHED BY ALFRED A. KNOPF AND ALFRED A. KNOPF CANADA

Library of Congress Cataloging-in-Publication Data
Armstrong, Karen, [date]
Twelve steps to a compassionate life / Karen Armstrong.
p. cm.
"A Borzoi book."
Includes bibliographical references.
ISBN 978-0-307-59559-1
1. Compassion. 2. Twelve-step programs. I. Title.
BJ1475.A77 2010
177'.7—dc22   2010036870

Library and Archives Canada Cataloguing in Publication
Armstrong, Karen, [date]
Twelve steps to a compassionate life / Karen Armstrong.
Issued also in electronic format.
ISBN 978-0-307-40065-9
1. Compassion—Religious aspects. 2. Conduct of life. I. Title.
BL624.A74 2010   204'.4   C2010-904191-7

Jacket design by Mary Jane Callister

Manufactured in the United States of America
Published January 11, 2011
Reprinted Two Times
Fourth Printing, May 2011

For Amy Novogratz

CONTENTS

TWELVE STEPS

TO A

COMPASSIONATE LIFE

Wish for a Better World

In November 2007, I heard that I had won a prize. Each year TED (the acronym for Technology, Entertainment, Design), a private nonprofit organization best known for its superb conferences on "ideas worth spreading," gives awards to people whom they think have made a difference but who, with their help, could make even more of an impact. Other winners have included former U.S. president Bill Clinton, the scientist E. O. Wilson, and the British chef Jamie Oliver. The recipient is given $100,000 and, more importantly, is granted a wish for a better world. I knew immediately what I wanted. One of the chief tasks of our time must surely be to build a global community in which all peoples can live together in mutual respect; yet religion, which should be making a major contribution, is seen as part of the problem. All faiths insist that compassion is the

{ 3 }

test of true spirituality and that it brings us into relation with the transcendence we call God, Brahman, Nirvana, or Dao. Each has formulated its own version of what is sometimes called the Golden Rule, "Do not treat others as you would not like them to treat you," or in its positive form, "Always treat others as you would wish to be treated yourself." Further, they all insist that you cannot confine your benevolence to your own group; you must have concern for everybody—even your enemies.

Yet sadly we hear little about compassion these days. I have lost count of the number of times I have jumped into a London taxi and, when the cabbie asks how I make a living, have been informed categorically that religion has been the cause of all the major wars in history. In fact, the causes of conflict are usually greed, envy, and ambition, but in an effort to sanitize them, these self-serving emotions have often been cloaked in religious rhetoric. There has been much flagrant abuse of religion in recent years. Terrorists have used their faith to justify atrocities that violate its most sacred values. In the Roman Catholic Church, popes and bishops have ignored the suffering of countless women and children by turning a blind eye to the sexual abuse committed by their priests. Some religious leaders seem to behave like secular politicians, singing the praises of their own denomination and decrying their rivals with scant regard for charity. In their public pronouncements, they rarely speak of compassion but focus instead on such secondary matters as sexual practices, the ordination of women, or abstruse doctrinal definitions, implying that a correct stance on these issues—rather than the Golden Rule—is the criterion of true faith.

Yet it is hard to think of a time when the compassionate voice of religion has been so sorely needed. Our world is dangerously polarized. There is a worrying imbalance of power and wealth and, as a result, a growing rage, malaise, alienation, and humiliation that have erupted in terrorist atrocities that endanger us all. We are engaged in wars that we seem unable either to end or to win. Disputes that were secular in origin, such as the Arab-Israeli conflict, have been allowed to fester and become "holy," and once they have been sacralized, positions tend to harden and become resistant to pragmatic solutions. And yet at the same time we are bound together more closely than ever before through the electronic media. Suffering and want are no longer confined to distant, disadvantaged parts of the globe. When stocks plummet in one country, there is a domino effect in markets all around the world. What happens today in Gaza or Afghanistan is now likely to have repercussions tomorrow in London or New York. We all face the terrifying possibility of environmental catastrophe. In a world in which small groups will increasingly have powers of destruction hitherto confined to the nation-state, it has become imperative to apply the Golden Rule globally, ensuring that all peoples are treated as we would wish to be treated ourselves. If our religious and ethical traditions fail to address this challenge, they will fail the test of our time.

So at the award ceremony in February 2008, I asked TED to help me create, launch, and propagate a Charter for Compassion that would be written by leading thinkers from a variety of major faiths and would restore compassion to the heart of religious and moral life. The charter would counter the voices of extremism, intolerance, and hatred. At a time when religions are widely assumed to be at loggerheads, it would also show that, despite our significant differences, on this we are all in agreement and that it is indeed possible for the religious to reach across the divide and work together for justice and peace.

Thousands of people from all over the world contributed to a draft charter on a multilingual website in Hebrew, Arabic, Urdu, Spanish, and English; their comments were presented to the Council of Conscience, a group of notable individuals from six faith traditions (Judaism, Christianity, Islam, Hinduism, Buddhism, and Confucianism), who met in Switzerland in February 2009 to compose the final version:

> The principle of compassion lies at the heart of all religious, ethical and spiritual traditions, calling us always to treat all others as we wish to be treated ourselves.

> Compassion impels us to work tirelessly to alleviate the suffering of our fellow creatures, to dethrone ourselves from the centre of our world and put another there, and to honour the inviolable sanctity of every single human being, treating everybody, without exception, with absolute justice, equity and respect.

It is also necessary in both public and private life to refrain consistently and empathically from inflicting pain. To act or speak violently out of spite, chauvinism or self-interest, to impoverish, exploit or deny basic rights to anybody, and to incite hatred by denigrating others—even our enemies—is a denial of our common humanity. We acknowledge that we have failed to live compassionately and that some have even increased the sum of human misery in the name of religion.

We therefore call upon all men and women

❦ to restore compassion to the centre of morality and religion;

❦ to return to the ancient principle that any interpretation of scripture that breeds violence, hatred or disdain is illegitimate;

❦ to ensure that youth are given accurate and respectful information about other traditions, religions and cultures;

❦ to encourage a positive appreciation of cultural and religious diversity;

❦ to cultivate an informed empathy with the suffering of all human beings—even those regarded as enemies.

We urgently need to make compassion a clear, luminous and dynamic force in our polarized world. Rooted in a principled determination to transcend selfishness, compassion can break down political, dogmatic, ideological and religious boundaries. Born of our deep interdependence, compassion is essential to human relationships and to a fulfilled humanity. It is the path to enlightenment, and indispensible to the creation of a just economy and a peaceful global community.

The charter was launched on November 12, 2009, in sixty different locations throughout the world; it was enshrined in synagogues, mosques, temples, and churches as well as in such secular institutions as the Karachi Press Club and the Sydney Opera House. But the work is only just beginning. At this writing, we have more than 150 partners working together throughout the globe to translate the charter into practical, realistic action.[1]

But can compassion heal the seemingly intractable problems of our time? Is this virtue even feasible in the technological age? And what does "compassion" actually mean? Our English word is often confused with "pity" and associated with an uncritical, sentimental benevolence: the *Oxford English Dictionary,* for example, defines "compassionate" as "piteous" or "pitiable." This perception of compassion is not only widespread but ingrained. When I gave a lecture in the Netherlands recently, I emphatically made the point that compassion did *not* mean feeling sorry for people; nevertheless, the Dutch translation of my text in the newspaper *De Volkskrant* consistently rendered "compassion" as "pity." But "compassion" derives from the Latin *patiri* and the Greek *pathein,* meaning "to suffer, undergo, or experience." So "*com*passion" means "to endure [something] *with* another person," to put ourselves in somebody else's shoes, to feel her pain as though it were our own, and to enter generously into his point of view. That is why compassion is aptly summed up in the Golden Rule, which asks us to look into our own hearts, discover what gives us pain, and then refuse, under any circumstance whatsoever, to inflict that pain on anybody else. Compassion can be defined, therefore, as an attitude of principled, consistent altruism.

The first person to formulate the Golden Rule, as far as we know, was the Chinese sage Confucius (551–479 BCE),[*] who when asked which of his teachings his disciples could practice "all day and every day" replied: "Perhaps the saying about *shu* ('consideration'). Never do to others what you would not like them to do to you."[2] This, he said, was the thread that ran right through the spiritual method he called the Way (*dao*) and pulled all its teachings together. "Our Master's Way," explained one of his pupils, "is nothing but this: doing-your-best-for-others (*zhong*) and consideration (*shu*)."[3] A better translation of *shu* is "likening to oneself"; people should not put themselves in a special, privileged category but relate their own experience to that of others "all day and every day." Confucius called this ideal

---

[*]Throughout I use BCE (Before the Common Era) and CE (Common Era), as they are more inclusive than the Christian BC and AD.

ren, a word that originally meant "noble" or "worthy" but that by his time simply meant "human." Some scholars have argued that its root meaning was "softness," "pliability."[4] But Confucius always refused to define *ren,* because, he said, it did not adequately correspond to any of the familiar categories of his day.[5] It could be understood only by somebody who practiced it perfectly and was inconceivable to anybody who did not. A person who behaved with *ren* "all day and every day" would become a *junzi,* a "mature human being."

Compassion, therefore, was inseparable from humanity; instead of being motivated by self-interest, a truly humane person was consistently oriented toward others. The disciplined practice of *shu* took you into a dimension of experience that was transcendent because it went beyond the egotism that characterizes most human transactions. The Buddha (c. 470–390 BCE) would have agreed.[6] He claimed to have discovered a realm of sacred peace within himself that he called *nirvana* ("blowing out"), because the passions, desires, and selfishness that had hitherto held him in thrall had been extinguished like a flame. Nirvana, he claimed, was an entirely natural state and could be achieved by anybody who put his regimen into practice. One of its central disciplines was a meditation on four elements of the "immeasurable" love that exists within everyone and everything: *maitri* ("loving kindness"), the desire to bring happiness to all sentient beings; *karuna* ("compassion"), the resolve to liberate all creatures from their pain; *mudita* ("sympathetic joy"), which takes delight in the happiness of others; and finally *upeksha* ("even-mindedness"), an equanimity that enables us to love all beings equally and impartially.

These traditions, therefore, agree that compassion is natural to human beings, that it is the fulfillment of human nature, and that in calling us to set ego aside in a consistently empathetic consideration of others, it can introduce us to a dimension of existence that transcends our normal self-bound state. Later, as we shall see, the three monotheistic religions would arrive at similar conclusions, and the fact that this ideal surfaced in all these faiths independently suggests that it reflects something essential to the structure of our humanity.

Compassion is something that we recognize and admire; it has resonated with human beings throughout history, and when we encounter a truly compassionate man or woman we feel enhanced. The names of the Quaker prison reformer Elizabeth Fry (1780–1845), Florence Nightingale (1820–1910), the hospital reformer, and Dorothy Day (1897–1980), founder of the Catholic Worker movement, have all become bywords for heroic philanthropy. Despite the fact that they were women in an aggressively male society, all three succeeded in making the compassionate ideal a practical, effective, and enduring force in a world that was in danger of forgetting it. The immense public veneration of Mahatma Gandhi (1869–1948), Martin Luther King Jr. (1929–68), Nelson Mandela, and the Dalai Lama shows that people are hungry for a more compassionate and principled form of leadership. On a different level, the popular cult of the late Diana, Princess of Wales and the extravagant displays of grief after her death in 1997 suggest that, despite her personal difficulties, her warm, hands-on approach was experienced as a welcome contrast to the more distant and impersonal manner of other public figures.

But in many ways compassion is alien to our modern way of life. The capitalist economy is intensely competitive and individualistic, and goes out of its way to encourage us to put ourselves first. When he developed his theory of the evolution of species, Charles Darwin (1809–82) revealed a nature that, as Tennyson had already suggested, was "red in tooth and claw"; the biologist Herbert Spencer (1820–1903) believed that, instead of being imbued with Buddhist "love" or the "softness" of *ren,* all creatures were perpetually engaged in a brutal struggle in which only the fittest survived. Because it runs counter to the Darwinian vision, advocates of evolutionary theory since Thomas H. Huxley (1825–95) have found altruism problematic. Today positivists, who believe science to be the sole criterion of truth, have argued that our genes are inescapably selfish and that we are programmed to pursue our own interests at whatever cost to our rivals. We *have* to put ourselves first. Altruism is, therefore, an illusion, a pious dream that is unnatural to humanity. At best it is a "meme," a unit of cultural ideas, symbols, or practices, that has colonized our minds. A "blessed" misfiring of natural selection, it has turned out to be a useful survival mechanism for *Homo sapiens,* because those groups that learned to cooperate forged ahead in the desperate competition for resources.[7] But this so-called altruism, they insist, is only apparent; it too is ultimately selfish. "The 'altruist' expects reciprocation for himself and his closest relatives," E. O. Wilson has argued. "His good behavior is calculating, often in a wholly conscious way, and his maneuvers are orchestrated by the excruciatingly intricate sanctions and demands of society." Such "soft-core altruism" is characterized by "lying, pretense, and deceit, including self-deceit, because the actor is more convincing who believes that his performance is real."[8]

There is no doubt that in the deepest recess of their minds, men and women are indeed ruthlessly selfish. This egotism is rooted in the "old brain," which was bequeathed to us by the reptiles that struggled out of the primal slime some 500 million years ago. Wholly intent on personal survival, these creatures were motivated by mechanisms that neuroscientists have called the "Four Fs": feeding, fighting, fleeing, and—for want of a more basic word—reproduction. These drives fanned out into fast-acting systems, alerting reptiles to compete pitilessly for food, to ward off any threat, to dominate their territory, seek a place of safety, and perpetuate their genes. Our reptilian ancestors were, therefore, interested only in status, power, control, territory, sex, personal gain, and survival. *Homo sapiens* inherited these neurological systems; they are located in the hypothalamus at the base of the brain, and it is thanks to them that our species survived. The emotions they engender are strong, automatic, and "all about me."

Over the millennia, however, human beings also evolved a "new brain," the neocortex, home of the reasoning powers that enable us to reflect on the world and on ourselves, and to stand back from these instinctive, primitive passions. But the Four Fs continue to inform all our activities. We are still programmed to acquire more and more goods, to respond instantly to any threat, and to fight mercilessly for the survival of number one. These instincts are overwhelming and automatic; they are meant to override our more rational considerations. We are *supposed* to throw our book aside and flee if a tiger suddenly appears in the garden. But our two brains coexist uneasily: it has been fatal when humans have employed their new-brain capacities to enhance and promote old-brain motivation; when, for example, we have created technology able to destroy the enemies that threaten us on an unprecedented scale.[9]

So are the positivists correct in their claim that our compassion is skin-deep? Much of the twentieth century was certainly red in tooth and claw, and already the Four Fs have been much in evidence in the twenty-first. Compassion has dropped so far out of sight these days that many are confused about what is required. It even inspires overt hostility. The controversy surrounding Mother Teresa of Calcutta (1910–97) shows how difficult it could be for a relatively unsophisticated woman, who is making a heroic effort to address a crying need, to find her way through the labyrinthine and often corrupt world of twentieth-century politics. The vitriol of some of her critics reveals not only an uncompassionate tendency in modern discourse—are we not all flawed beings?—but also a visceral distaste for the compassionate ethos and a principled determination to expose any manifestation of it as "lying, pretense, and deceit." Many people today, it seems, would rather be *right* than compassionate.

And yet human beings continue to endorse ideologies that promote a principled, selfless empathy. Auguste Comte (1798–1857), the founder of positivism who also coined the term "altruism," saw no incompatibility between compassion and the scientific era he hailed with such enthusiasm. Even though he had lived through a terrifying period of revolution in Europe, he looked forward confidently to the dawning of an enlightened social order in which cooperation between people would be based not on coercion but on

> their own inherent tendency to universal love. No calculations of self-interest can rival this social instinct, whether in promptitude of breadth of intuition, or in boldness and tenacity of purpose. True it is that the benevolent emotions have in most cases less intrinsic energy than the selfish. But they have this beautiful quality, that social life not only permits their growth, but stimulates it to an almost unlimited extent, while it holds their antagonists in constant check.[10]

Unlike E. O. Wilson, Comte did not regard compassionate behavior as hypocritical and calculated. Instead, he linked the "benevolent emotions" with the aesthetic, convinced that their "beautiful quality" had a power of its own.

The very first extant documents of *Homo sapiens* indicate that we devised art forms at the same time and for many of the same reasons as we created religious systems. Our neocortex has made us meaning-seeking creatures, acutely aware of the perplexity and tragedy of our predicament, and if we do not discover some ultimate significance in our lives, we fall easily into despair. In art as in religion, we find a means of letting go and encouraging the "softness" and "pliability" that draw us toward the other; art and religion both propel us into a new place within ourselves, where we find a degree of serenity. The earliest cave paintings created by our Palaeolithic ancestors some thirty thousand years ago in southern France and northern Spain almost certainly had a ritual function. From the very beginning, therefore, art and religion were allied. These frescoes and engravings have an aesthetic power that still evokes awe in visitors. Their depiction of the animals on whom these hunting communities were entirely dependent has a numinous quality; intent as they were on the acquisition of food—the first of the Four Fs—the ferocity of the hunters was tempered by a manifest tenderness toward and affinity with the beasts they were obliged to kill.

The vision that inspired the cave paintings so long ago may have been similar to the spirituality of modern indigenous hunting communities.[11] These tribesmen are disturbed by the fact that their lives depend on the slaughter of the animals they regard as friends and patrons, and they assuage their anxiety in rituals that evoke respect for and empathy with their prey. In the Kalahari Desert, for example, where wood is scarce, Bushmen rely on light weapons that can only graze the surface of the skin, so they anoint their arrows with a poison that kills the animal very slowly. The hunter has to remain with his victim during its last days—crying when it cries out, shuddering when it trembles, and entering symbolically into its death throes.

In recent years, anthropologists, ethologists, and neuroscientists have all researched the development in the animal and human brain of these "benevolent" emotions, which, they argue, have made our thought patterns more flexible, creative, and intelligent.[12] In 1878, the French anatomist Paul Broca discovered that all mammals had a section of the brain that seemed older than the neocortex but was not present in the reptilian brain. He called this intermediate region *le grand lobe limbique*.[13] Building on this insight during the 1950s, Paul MacLean, physician and neuroscientist at the U.S. National Institute of Mental Health, suggested that the positive emotions of compassion, joy, serenity, and maternal affection did not emanate from the hypothalamus, as assumed hitherto, but from the limbic system, which he located beneath the cortex.[14] As a further refinement, during the 1960s Roger Sperry of the California Institute of Technology researched the differences between our right and left brains: while the left brain reasons, explains, and analyzes and is concerned with words, distinctions, precision, and cause and effect, the right brain emotes, weeps, responds to symbolism, and is the home of art, music, and the "softer," more "pliable" emotions.[15] It seems, therefore, that the more aggressive instincts of the hypothalamus exist alongside other brain systems that make empathy possible and that we are hardwired for compassion as well as for cruelty.

The arrival of warm-blooded mammals led to the evolution of a brain that was able to care for others and thus help to ensure the survival of their young. At first this care was rudimentary and automatic; but over millennia, mammals began to build nests for their infants and learned to behave in a way that would ensure their health and development. For the first time, sentient beings were developing the capacity to protect, nurture, and nourish a creature other than themselves. Over millions of years, this strategy proved so successful in establishing genetic lineages that it led to the evolution of still more complex brain systems.[16] The process seems to have been symbiotic. In order to accommodate these new skills, the brains of mammals got bigger; this meant that increasingly their young had to be born prematurely so that they could pass through the birth canal; the infants were, therefore, helpless and needed the support, care, and protection not only of their parents but of the entire community.[17] This was especially true of *Homo sapiens,* which had evolved an enormous brain. Because his mother had no fur, the human baby could not cling to her; instead, she had to clasp and carry him for hours at a time, subordinating her own hunger, needs, and desires to his in a process that was no longer automatic but emotionally motivated and, to a degree, voluntary. But parental affection ensured the survival of the species, helped the young to thrive, and taught humans to develop other alliances and friendships that were extremely useful in the struggle for survival. Gradually they developed the capacity for altruism.[18]

When animals are not warding off threats or engrossed in the quest for food, they relax and become content. A soothing regulatory system takes over, balancing the systems that control the response to threat and hunger, so that they can take time out and allow their bodies to repair themselves. It used to be thought that this quiescence was simply the result of the more aggressive drives zoning out, but it has now been found that this physical relaxation is also accompanied in both mammals and humans by profound and positive feelings of peace, security, and well-being.[19] Produced initially by maternal soothing, these emotions are activated by such hormones as oxytocin, which induces a sense of closeness to others and plays a crucial role in the development of parental attachment.[20] When human beings entered this peaceful state of mind, they were liberated from anxiety and could, therefore, think more clearly and have fresh insights; as they acquired new skills and had more leisure, some sought to reproduce this serenity in activities, disciplines, and rituals that were found to induce it.

In Semitic languages, the word for "compassion" (*rahamanut* in post-biblical Hebrew and *rahman* in Arabic), is related etymologically to *rehem/RHM* ("womb"). The icon of mother and child is an archetypal expression of human love. It evokes the maternal affection that in all likelihood gave birth to our capacity for unselfish, unconditional altruism. It may well be that the experience of teaching, guiding, soothing, protecting, and nourishing their young taught men and women how to look after people other than their own kin, developing a concern that was not based on cold calculation but imbued with warmth. We humans are more radically dependent on love than any other species. Our brains have evolved to be caring and to need care—to such an extent that they are impaired if this nurture is lacking.[21] Mother love involves affective love; it has a powerful hormonal base, but it also requires dedicated, unselfish action "all day and every day." A mother's concern for her child pervades all her activities. Whether she feels like it or not, she has to get up to her crying infant night after night, watch him at every moment of the day, and learn to control her own exhaustion, impatience, anger, and frustration. She is tied to her child long after he has reached adulthood; indeed, on both sides, the relationship is usually terminated only at death. Maternal love can be heartbreaking as well as fulfilling; it requires stamina, fortitude, and a strong degree of selflessness.

We know from our own experience that human beings do not confine their altruistic behavior to those who carry their genes. The Confucian philosopher Mencius (c. 371–c. 289 BCE) was convinced that nobody was wholly without sympathy for other people. If you saw a child poised perilously on the edge of a well, you would immediately lunge forward to save her. Your action is not inspired by self-interest: you would not pause to ascertain whether or not she was related to you; you were not motivated by the desire to ingratiate yourself with her parents or win the admiration of your friends, or by the fact that you were irritated by her cries for help. There was no time for such calculation; you would simply feel her plight in your gut. There would be something disturbingly wrong with a person who watched the child fall to her death without a flicker of unease. Firefighters regularly plunge into burning houses to rescue people who are entirely unknown to them; volunteers risk their lives to rescue climbers stranded on mountainsides; and we have all heard stories of passersby who save total strangers from drowning, often insisting that there was nothing heroic about it: "I could do nothing else," they will say. "I could no more have let go of his hand than cut off my own." Some researchers attribute this response to the "mirror neurons" in the frontal region of the brain, which light up on the neuroimagist's screen when the subject watches somebody else burning her hand. These recently discovered neurons seem to mediate empathy and enable us to feel the pain of another as if it were our own—simply by watching her experience it.[22] You could stamp on this natural shoot of compassion, Mencius argued, just as you can cripple or deform your body, but if you cultivate this altruistic tendency assiduously, it will acquire a dynamic power of its own.[23]

The religious systems have all discovered that it is indeed possible to nourish the shoots of compassion described by Mencius and learn to withstand the me-first mechanisms of the old reptilian brain. Human beings have always been prepared to work hard to enhance a natural ability. We doubtless learned to run and jump in order to escape from our predators, but from these basic skills we developed ballet and gymnastics: after years of dedicated practice men and women acquire the ability to move with unearthly grace and achieve physical feats that are impossible for an untrained body. We devised language to improve communications and now we have poetry, which pushes speech into another dimension. In the same way, those who have persistently trained themselves in the art of compassion manifest new capacities in the human heart and mind; they discover that when they reach out consistently toward others, they are able to live with the suffering that inevitably comes their way with serenity, kindness, and creativity. They find that they have a new clarity and experience a richly intensified state of being.

The Four Fs are powerful; they can overturn all our efforts to live more kindly and rationally in a second, but we are thinking beings, with a fully developed neocortex, and have the ability to take responsibility for them. Indeed, we have a duty to protect ourselves and others from our more destructive instincts. Do we want to succumb to our reptilian brain, when we have seen for ourselves what can happen when hatred, disgust, greed, or the desire for vengeance consume entire groups? In our perilously divided world, compassion is in our best interest. To acquire it, however, will demand an immense effort of mind and heart. Gandhi memorably said that we must ourselves become the change that we wish to see in the world. We cannot reasonably expect the leaders of our own or other people's nations to adopt more humane policies if we ourselves continue to live egotistically, unkindly, and greedily, and give free rein to unexamined prejudice. We cannot demand that our enemies become more tolerant and less violent if we make no effort to transcend the Four Fs in our own lives. We have a natural capacity for compassion as well as for cruelty. We can either emphasize those aspects of our traditions, religious or secular, that speak of hatred, exclusion, and suspicion, *or* work with those that stress the interdependence and equality of all human beings. The choice is ours.

People often ask: "How do we start?" The demands of compassion seem so daunting that it is difficult to know where to begin—hence this twelve-step program. It will immediately bring to mind the twelve steps of Alcoholics Anonymous. We are addicted to our egotism. We cannot think how we would manage without our pet hatreds and prejudices that give us such a buzz of righteousness; like addicts, we have come to depend on the instant rush of energy and delight we feel when we display our cleverness by making an unkind remark and the spurt of triumph when we vanquish an annoying colleague. Thus do we assert ourselves and tell the world who we are. It is difficult to break a habit upon which we depend for our sense of self. As in AA, the disciplines learned at each step in this program have to become a part of your life.

I wrote the first version of these twelve steps as a "vook," a cross between a video and a book, to be read electronically. The printed book, however, is a very different medium, and I have been able here to explore these themes in more detail and at greater depth. In the vook, I was encouraged to keep historical reference to a minimum and concentrate on the present. But I am a religious historian, and it is my study of the spiritualities of the past that has taught me all I know about compassion. I think that in this respect the faith traditions still have a great deal to teach us. But it is important to say that the twelve-step program does not depend on supernatural or creedal convictions. I am in agreement with His Holiness the Dalai Lama that "whether a person is a religious believer does not matter much. Far more important is that they be a good human being."[24] At their best, all religious, philosophical, and ethical traditions are based on the principle of compassion.

I suggest that you begin by reading the entire program all the way through to see where you are headed, then return to work on the first step. Each step will build on the disciplines practiced and the habits acquired in those that have gone before. The effect will be cumulative. Do not skip any of the steps, because each one is an indispensable part of the process. And do not leave a step until the recommended practices have become part of your daily routine. There is no hurry. We are not going to develop an impartial, universal love overnight. These days we often expect things to happen immediately. We want instant transformation and instant enlightenment—hence the popularity of those television makeover shows that create a new garden, a new room, or a new face in a matter of days. But it takes longer to reorient our minds and hearts; this type of transformation is slow, undramatic, and incremental. Each step asks more—and more—and more. If you follow the program step by step, you will find that you are beginning to see the world, yourself, and other people in a different light.

Learn About Compassion

All twelve steps will be educative in the deepest sense; the Latin *educere* means "to lead out," and this program is designed to bring forth the compassion that, as we have seen, exists potentially within every human being so that it can become a healing force in our own lives and in the world. We are trying to retrain our responses and form mental habits that are kinder, gentler, and less fearful of others. Reading and learning about compassion will be an important part of the process and should become a lifetime habit, but it does not stop there. You cannot learn to drive by reading the car manual; you have to get into the vehicle and practice manipulating it until the skills you acquire so laboriously become second nature. You cannot learn to swim by sitting on the side of the pool watching others cavort in the water; you have to take the plunge and learn to float. If you persevere, you will acquire an ability that at first seemed impossible. It is the same with compassion; we can learn about the neurological makeup of the brain and the requirements of our tradition, but until and unless we actually modify our behavior and learn to think and act toward others in accordance with the Golden Rule, we will make no progress.

As an initial step, it might be helpful as a symbolic act of commitment to visit www.charterforcompassion.org and register with the Charter for Compassion. The charter is essentially a summons to compassionate action, and the website will enable you to keep up, week by week, with the charter's progress in various parts of the world. But the charter was a joint document that does not reflect the vision of a particular tradition, so it is important to integrate it with a mythos that will motivate you. No teaching that is simply a list of directives can be effective. We need inspiration and motivation that reach a level of the mind that is deeper than the purely rational and touch the emotions rooted in the limbic region of the brain. It is therefore important to explore your own tradition, be it religious or secular, and seek out its teaching about compassion. This will speak to you in a way that is familiar; resonate with some of your deepest aspirations, hopes, and fears; and explain what this journey toward compassion will entail.

In the Suggestions for Further Reading at the back of the book, you will find titles that will help you expand your knowledge about your own and other people's traditions. You might find it useful to form a reading discussion group with whom you can go through the twelve steps. It might be interesting to include people from different religious and secular traditions, since the comparative study of other faiths and ideologies can enrich your understanding of your own. You might also like to keep a private anthology of passages or poems that you find particularly inspiring and make notes of what you have learned about the mythos that introduces us to the deeper meaning of compassion.

The concept of mythology needs explanation because in our modern scientific world it has lost much of its original force. A myth is not a fanciful fairy tale. In popular speech the word "myth" is often used to describe something that is simply not true. Accused of a peccadillo in his past life, a politician is likely to protest that the story is a myth—that it didn't happen. But in the premodern world, the purpose of myth was not to impart factual or historical information. The Greek *mythos* derives from the verb *musteion,* "to close the mouth or the eyes." It is associated with silence, obscurity, and darkness. A myth was an attempt to express some of the more elusive aspects of life that cannot easily be expressed in logical, discursive speech. A myth is *more* than history; it is an attempt to explain the deeper significance of an event. A myth has been well described as something that in some sense happened once—but that also happens all the time. It is about timeless, universal truth.

If somebody had asked the ancient Greeks whether they believed that there was sufficient historical evidence for the famous story of Demeter, goddess of harvest and grain, and her beloved daughter, Persephone (Was Persephone really abducted by Hades and imprisoned in the underworld? Did Demeter truly secure her release? How could you prove that Persephone returned to the upper world each year?), they would have found these questions obtuse. The truth of the myth, they might have replied, was evident for all to see: it was clear in the way that the world came to life each spring, in the recurrent burgeoning of the harvest, and, above all, in the profound truth that death and life are inseparable. There is no new life if the seed does not go down into the ground and die; you cannot have life without death. The rituals associated with the myth, which were performed annually at Eleusis (where Demeter is said to have stayed during her search for Persephone), were carefully crafted to help people accept their mortality; afterward many found that they could contemplate the prospect of their own death with greater equanimity.[1]

A myth, therefore, makes sense only if it is translated into action—either ritually or behaviorally. It is comprehensible only if it is imparted as part of a process of transformation.[2] Myth has been aptly described as an early form of psychology. The tales about gods threading their way through labyrinths or fighting with monsters were describing an archetypal truth rather than an actual occurrence. Their purpose was to introduce the audience to the labyrinthine world of the psyche, showing them how to negotiate this mysterious realm and grapple with their own demons. The myth of the hero told people what they had to do to unlock their own heroic potential. When Sigmund Freud and C. G. Jung charted their modern scientific exploration of the psyche, they turned instinctively to these ancient narratives. A myth could put you in the correct spiritual posture, but it was up to you to take the next step. In our scientifically oriented world, we look for solid information and have lost the older art of interpreting these emblematic stories of gods walking out of tombs or seas splitting asunder, and this has made religion problematic. Without practical implementation, a myth can remain as opaque and abstract as the rules of a board game, which sound complicated and dull until you pick up the dice and start to play; then everything immediately falls into place and makes sense. As we go through the steps, we will examine some of the traditional myths to discover what they teach about the compassionate imperative—and how we must act in order to integrate them with our own lives.

It is not possible here to give an exhaustive account of the teachings of all the major traditions. I have had to concentrate on a few of the seminal prophets and sages who developed this ethos. But this brief overview can give us some idea of the universality of the compassionate ideal and the circumstances in which it came to birth.

We have seen that there are brain mechanisms and hormones that induce such positive emotions as love, compassion, gratitude, and forgiveness but that they are not as powerful as the more primitive instinctual reflexes known as the Four Fs located in our reptilian old brain. But the great sages understood that it was possible to reorient the mind, and by putting some distance between their thinking selves and these potentially destructive instincts they found new peace. They did not come to this insight on lonely mountaintops or in desert fastnesses. They were all living in societies not unlike our own, which witnessed intense political conflict and fundamental social change. In every case, the catalyst for major spiritual change was a principled revulsion from the violence that had reached unprecedented heights as a result of this upheaval.[3] These new spiritualities came into being at a time when the old brain was being co-opted by the calculating, rational new brain in ways that were exciting and life-enhancing but that many found profoundly disturbing.

For millennia, human beings had lived in small isolated groups and tribes, using their rational powers to organize their society efficiently. At a time when survival depended on the sharing of limited resources, a reputation for altruism and generosity as well as physical strength and wisdom may well have been valued in a tribal leader. If you had not shared your resources in a time of plenty, who would help you and your people in your hour of need? The clan would survive only if members subordinated their personal desires to the requirements of the group and were ready to lay down their lives for the sake of the whole community. It was necessary for humans to become a positive presence in the minds of others, even when they were absent.[4] It was important to elicit affection and concern in other members of the tribe so that they would come back and search for you if you were lost or wounded during a hunting expedition. But the Four Fs were also crucial to the tribal ethos, as essential for the group as for the individual. Hence tribalism often exhibited an aggressive territorialism, desire for status, reflexive loyalty to the leader and the group, suspicion of outsiders, and a ruthless determination to acquire more and more resources, even if this meant that other groups would starve. Tribalism was probably essential to the survival of *Homo sapiens*, but it could become problematic when human beings acquired the technology to make deadlier weapons and began to compete for territory and resources on a larger scale. It did not disappear when human beings began to build cities and nations. It surfaces even today in sophisticated, wealthy societies that have no doubts about their survival.

But as human beings became more secure, achieved greater control over their environment, and began to build towns and cities, some had the leisure to explore the interior life and find ways of controlling their destructive impulses. From about 900 to 200 BCE, during what the German philosopher Karl Jaspers called the "Axial Age," there occurred a religious revolution that proved pivotal to the spiritual development of humanity. In four distinct regions, sages, prophets, and mystics began to develop traditions that have continued to nourish men and women: Hinduism, Buddhism, and Jainism on the Indian subcontinent; Confucianism and Daoism in China; monotheism in the Middle East; and philosophical rationalism in Greece.[5] This was the period of the Upanishads, the Buddha, Confucius, Laozi, Isaiah, Ezekiel, Ezra, Socrates, and Aeschylus. We have never surpassed the insights of the Axial Age. In times of spiritual and social crisis, people have repeatedly turned back to it for guidance. They may have interpreted the Axial discoveries differently, but they never succeeded in going beyond them. Rabbinic Judaism, Christianity, and Islam, for example, were all latter-day flowerings of this original vision, which they translated marvelously into an idiom that spoke directly to the troubled circumstances of a later period. Compassion would be a key element in each of these movements.

The Aryan peoples of India would always be in the vanguard of this spiritual and psychological transformation and would develop a particularly sophisticated understanding of the workings of the mind. Aggressive, passionate warriors addicted to raiding and rustling the cattle of neighboring groups, the Aryan tribes, who had settled in what is now the Punjab, had sacralized their violence. Their religious rituals included the sacrificial slaughter of animals, fierce competitions, and mock raids and battles in which participants were often injured or even killed. But in the ninth century BCE, priests began systematically to extract this aggression from the liturgy, transforming these dangerous rites into more anodyne ceremonies. Eventually they managed to persuade the warriors to give up their sacred war games. As these ritual specialists began to investigate the causes of violence in the psyche, they initiated a spiritual awakening.[6] From a very early date, therefore, they had espoused the ideal of *ahimsa* ("nonviolence") that would become central to Indian spirituality.

In the seventh century BCE, the sages who produced the earliest of the spiritual treatises known as the Upanishads took another important step forward. Instead of concentrating on the performance of external rites, they began to examine their interior significance. At this time Aryan society in the Ganges basin was in the early stages of urbanization.[7] The elite now had time to examine the inner workings of their minds—a luxury that had not been possible before humans were freed from the all-absorbing struggle for subsistence. The Brhadaranyaka Upanishad was probably composed in the kingdom of Videha, a frontier state on the most easterly point of Aryan expansion, where Aryans mixed with tribesmen from Iran as well as the indigenous peoples.[8] The early Upanishads reflect the intense excitement of these encounters. People thought nothing of traveling a thousand miles to consult a teacher, and kings and warriors debated the issues as eagerly as priests.

The sages and their pupils explored the complexity of the mind and had discovered the unconscious long before Jung and Freud; they were well aware of the effortless and reflexive drives of the human brain recently explored by neuroscientists. Above all, they were bent on finding the atman, the true "self" that was the source of all this mental activity and could not, therefore, be identical with the thoughts and feelings that characterize our ordinary mental and psychological experience. "You can't see the Seer, who does the seeing," explained Yajnavalkya, one of the most important of the early sages. "You can't hear the Hearer who does the hearing; you can't think with the Thinker who does the thinking; and you can't perceive the Perceiver who does the perceiving."[9] The sages were convinced that if they could access the innermost core of their being, they would achieve unity with the Brahman, "the All," the indestructible and imperishable energy that fuels the cosmos, establishes its laws, and pulls all the disparate parts of the universe together.[10]

The sages and their pupils claimed that their mental exercises, disciplined lifestyle, and intensely dialectical discussions had uncovered the atman and introduced them to a more potent mode of being. The way they described this experience suggests that it may have originated in the brain's soothing system, which takes over when an animal is at rest and free of threat. A person who knows the atman, said Yajnavalkya, is "calm, composed, cool, patient and collected." Above all, he is "free from fear," a phrase that runs like a thread through these texts.[11] But the peace discovered by the sages was more than bovine relaxation. They distinguished carefully and consistently between this new knowledge and a temporary, contingent contentment that is repeatedly overwhelmed by the Four Fs. The peaceful mood of a calf resting quietly beside his mother cannot withstand the incentive/resource-focused mechanism: when hungry, he reflexively leaps to his feet and roots around for food. If a lion appears on the scene, the threat-focused mechanism automatically fills him with the terror that will make him flee for his life. But the sages seem to have gained a more permanent degree of immunity from these instinctive drives. Once a person had accessed "the immense and unborn *atman,* un-ageing, undying, immortal and free from fear," he was free of terror and anxiety.[12] He was no longer so completely in thrall to the instinctual acquisitive drive that compelled him to want more and more, to pursue, desire, achieve, and consume: "A man who does not desire—who is freed from desires, whose desires are fulfilled, whose only desire is his *atman*—his vital functions do not depart. Brahman he is and to Brahman he goes."[13]

The sages did not see this state as supernatural; it

had not been bestowed upon them by a god but could be achieved by anybody who had the talent and tenacity to cultivate it, albeit with considerable expenditure of time and effort. A trainee ascetic had to study with his guru for as long as twelve years, and during this time his lifestyle was just as important as the intellectual content of his education. Enlightenment was impossible if he did not curb his aggressive, assertive ego, so he lived in a humble, self-effacing manner, tending his teacher's fire, collecting fuel from the forest, and begging for his food. All violence forbidden, he was expected to behave with detached courtesy to all. Even Indra, god of war, who never stopped boasting about his military and amorous exploits, had to study for 101 years with a human guru, giving up fighting and sex, cleaning his teacher's house, and tending his fire.[14] Once his training was complete, the student would go home, marry, and bring up his children, putting into practice everything that he had learned from his teacher: he would continue to study and meditate, forswear violence, and deal kindly and gently with others.[15]

As urbanization developed in India, the sages were disturbed by a new level of aggression. By the sixth century BCE, infant states were developing; these brought a degree of stability to the region, but the kings could impose order on their subjects only by means of their armies, which they also used to conquer more territory for themselves. The new market-based economy was fueled by greed, and bankers and merchants, locked in ceaseless competition, preyed ruthlessly on one another. To some, life seemed more violent than when cattle rustling had been the backbone of the economy. The old religion no longer spoke to the changing times. Increasingly people felt uneasy about the cruelty of animal sacrifice, which seemed at odds with the ideal of *ahimsa,* and looked instead to the "renouncers" (*samnyasins*), who had turned their back on society to craft an entirely different kind of humanity.

The mind-changing discipline of yoga had become central to Indian spirituality.[16] Classical yoga was not an aerobic exercise but a systematic assault on the ego. The word *yoga* ("yoking") is itself significant. It was originally used by the Aryans to describe the tethering of draft animals to the war chariot before a raid, but the new men of yoga were engaged in the conquest of inner space and in a raid on the unconscious drives that held human beings captive to their me-first instincts. In order to achieve an *ekstasis,* a "stepping outside" the norm, a yogi did the opposite of what came naturally. Instead of succumbing to the ceaseless motion that characterizes all sentient beings, he would sit as still as a plant or a statue. He controlled his respiration, the most fundamental and automatic of our physical functions, his aim being to stop breathing for as long as possible between exhalation and inhalation. He learned to master the ceaseless flux of thoughts, sensations, and fantasies that coursed through his mind in order to concentrate "on one point" (*ekagrata*). As a result, he found that he saw other objects and people differently; because he had repressed the aura of memory and personal association surrounding each one of them, he no longer saw them through the filter of his own desires and needs. The "I" was disappearing from his thinking.

But before he was permitted to practice the simplest yogic exercise, an aspiring yogi had to undergo a long apprenticeship, which amounted to a head-on collision with the Four Fs. He had to observe five "prohibitions" *(yamas)*. Violence of any sort was forbidden: he must not swat an insect, speak unkindly, make an irritable gesture, or harm a single creature in any way. Stealing was outlawed, which also meant that he could not grab food when he was hungry but must simply accept what he was given whenever it was offered. Renouncing the acquisitive drive, he forswore avarice and greed. He was required to speak the truth at all times, not altering what he said to protect himself or serve his own interests. And, finally, he had to abstain from sex and intoxicants, which could cloud his mind and hinder his yogic training. Until his guru was satisfied that this behavior was now second nature to him, he was not even allowed to sit in the yogic position. But once he had mastered these disciplines, explained Patanjali, author of the *Yoga Sutras,* he would experience "indescribable joy."[17] Making a deliberate effort to transcend the primitive self-protective instincts had propelled him into a different state of consciousness.

Siddhatta Gotama, the future Buddha, studied yoga under some of the best teachers of his day before he achieved the enlightenment of Nirvana. He quickly became expert, attaining the very highest states of trance. But he did not agree with the way his teachers interpreted these peak experiences. They told him that he had tasted the supreme enlightenment, but Gotama discovered that after the *ekstasis* had faded he was plagued by greed, lust, envy, and hatred in the same old way. He tried to extinguish these passions by practicing such fierce asceticism that he became horribly emaciated and almost ruined his health. Yet still his body clamored for attention. Finally, in a moment of mingled despair and defiance, he cried, "Surely there must be another way to enlightenment!" and at that moment a new solution declared itself to him.[18]

He recalled an incident from his early childhood, when his father had taken him to watch the ritual plowing of the fields before the first planting of the year. His nurse had left him under a rose-apple tree while she attended the ceremony, and little Gotama sat up and noticed that some tender shoots of young grass had been torn up by the plow and that the tiny insects clinging to them had been killed.[19] He felt a pang of grief as though his own relatives had died, and this moment of empathy took him out of himself, so that he achieved a "release of the mind" (ceto-vimutti). He felt a pure joy welling up from the depth of his being, sat in the yogic position, and, even though he had never had a yoga lesson in his short life, immediately entered a state of trance.

Looking back on that pivotal episode, Gotama realized that for those blessed moments his mind had been entirely free of greed, hatred, envy, and lust. So instead of trying to quench his humanity with harsh practices, he thought perhaps he should cultivate the emotions that had brought him ceto-vimutti: compassion, joy, and gratitude. He also realized that the five "prohibitions" should be balanced by their more positive counterparts. So instead of simply crushing his violent impulses, he would try to encourage feelings of loving kindness; instead of just refraining from lying, he would make sure that everything he said was "reasoned, accurate, clear and beneficial."[20] He would no longer be content to avoid theft, but would learn to take pleasure in the freedom he gained by possessing the bare minimum.

In order to enhance the natural impulse to empathy and compassion, Gotama developed a special form of meditation. In his yoga sessions, at each stage of his descent into the depths of his mind, he would contemplate what he called the "four immeasurable minds of love," that "huge, expansive and immeasurable feeling that knows no hatred," and direct them to the farthest corners of the world, not omitting a single creature from this radius of concern. First, he would evoke *maitri* ("loving kindness"), inducing in his mind an attitude of friendship for everything and everybody; next he meditated on *karuna* ("compassion"), desiring that all creatures be free of pain; third, he would bring to his mind *mudita*, the pure "joy" he had experienced under the rose-apple tree and that he now desired for all creatures; and finally he would try to free himself of personal attachment and partiality by loving all sentient beings with the "even-mindedness" of *upeksha*. Over time, by dint of disciplined practice, Gotama found that his mind broke free of the prism of selfishness and felt "expansive, without limits, enhanced, without hatred or petty malevolence."[21] He had understood that while spite, hatred, envy, and ingratitude shrink our horizons and limit our creativity, gratitude, compassion, and altruism broaden our perspective and break down the barricades we erect between ourselves and others in order to protect the frightened, greedy, insecure ego.[22]

The Buddha's crucial insight was that to live morally was to live for others. It was not enough simply to enjoy a religious experience. After enlightenment, he said, a person must return to the marketplace and there practice compassion to all, doing anything he or she could to alleviate the misery of other people. After achieving Nirvana, he had been tempted to luxuriate in the transcendent peace he had found, but instead he spent the remaining forty years of his life on the road teaching his method to others. In Mahayana Buddhism, the hero is the bodhisattva, who is on the brink of enlightenment but instead of disappearing into the bliss of Nirvana, decides to return to the suffering world: "We will become a shelter for the world, the world's place of rest, the final relief of the world, islands of the world, lights of the world, and the guides of the world's salvation"[23]

The Chinese sages focused less on the psychology of compassion and more on its potential social and political implications. In the West, Confucius is often seen as a petty-minded ritualist, obsessed with the minutiae of stultifying rules governing family life. He did indeed revive these ancient rites but saw them as a means of controlling egotism and cultivating compassion. These rituals (li) had been deliberately developed in the Yellow River basin during the eighth century BCE to moderate the extravagant behavior of the nobility. Aggressive deforestation had made more land available for cultivation but had destroyed the natural habitat of many species and decimated the region's wildlife.[24] Hunters now came home empty-handed, and because so much land was now devoted to growing crops, there was less for the breeding of sheep and cattle. In the old days, without a thought for the morrow, aristocrats had slaughtered hundreds of beasts and given lavish gifts to demonstrate their wealth. Concerned above all with status and prestige, they had engaged in bloody vendettas and petty feuds. But in the dawning age of scarcity, the new watchwords were moderation, control, and restraint. Court ritualists evolved complex codes to control every detail of life (even warfare was strictly governed by elaborate chivalric rites that mitigated the horror of battle).[25] The nobles discovered the virtue of self-restraint and no longer called out the army in response to every imagined slight.

For more than a century the *li* seemed to have worked.[26] But by the time of Confucius, the Four Fs had reasserted themselves. In the incipient market economy of the sixth century BCE, people were casting restraint to the winds in headlong and aggressive pursuit of luxury, wealth, and power. Large new states, ruled by erstwhile barbarians unfamiliar with the *li,* attacked the smaller principalities with impunity, resulting in terrible loss of life. Confucius was horrified. The Chinese seemed bent on self-destruction, and in his view, salvation lay in a renewed appreciation of the underlying spirit of the old rites. The rituals of consideration (*shu*) ensured that people did not treat others carelessly and were not driven simply by utility and self-interest; these gracious codes of behavior had made people conscious of the dignity of every human being; they expressed and conferred sacred respect; they taught every family member to live for the others; they introduced individuals to the virtue of "yielding" to their fellows, helping them to cultivate the "softness" and "pliability" of *ren*. Properly understood, therefore, the rites were a spiritual education that enabled people to transcend the limitations of selfishness. In the old days, it was thought that the *li* conferred a magical power on the recipient. Confucius reinterpreted this: when people are treated with reverence, they become conscious of their own sacred worth, and ordinary actions, such as eating and drinking, are lifted to a level higher than the biological and invested with holiness.

The implications for politics were immense. If instead of ruthlessly pursuing his own self-interest to the detriment of others, a ruler would "curb his ego and submit to *li* for a single day," Confucius believed, "everyone under Heaven would respond to his goodness!"[27] What is *ren,* asked one of his disciples, and how can it be applied to political life? In exactly the same way as you apply it to family life, Confucius replied: by treating everybody with respect.

> Behave away from home as though you were in the presence of an important guest. Deal with the common people as though you were officiating at an important sacrifice. Do not do to others what you would not like yourself. Then there will be no feelings of opposition to you, whether it is the affairs of a State that you are handling or the affairs of a Family.[28]

There would be no destructive wars if a ruler behaved toward other princes and states in this way; the Golden Rule would make it impossible to invade somebody else's territory because nobody would like this to happen to his own state. It was quite simple, Confucius explained to his outspoken pupil Zigong:

> As for *ren*, you yourself desire rank and standing; then help others to get rank and standing. You want to turn your merits to account; then help others to turn theirs to account—in fact, the ability to take one's own feelings as a guide—that is the sort of thing that lies in the direction of *ren*.[29]

Any ruler who behaved in this way, working for the true welfare of the people and laying his own interests aside, would become a force for great good in the world.

The family was the place where a *junzi* learned to live as a fully humane and mature person.[30] It was a school of compassion. But *ren* could not be confined to the family. In a vision that was not unlike the Buddha's, Confucius saw each person at the center of a constantly expanding series of concentric circles of compassion.[31] The lessons a *junzi* had learned from taking care of his parents, his wife, and his siblings would educate and enlarge his heart so that he felt empathy with more and more people: first with his city or village, then with his state, and finally with the entire world. The summons of *ren* was never ending. It was difficult because it required the abandonment of the vanity, resentment, and desire to dominate to which we are addicted.[32] And yet because *ren* was natural to us, an essential part of our humanity, it was easy. "Is *ren* so far away?" Confucius asked. "If we really wanted *ren,* we should find that it was at our very side."[33]

Those who followed his Way found that it transformed their lives, even though it was a lifelong struggle that would end only with death.[34] Confucius did not encourage speculation about what lay at the end of the Way; walking along the path of *shu* was itself a transcendent experience because, if practiced "all day and every day," it led to a continual *ekstasis* that left the grasping self behind. The dynamic nature of a life of *ren* was beautifully expressed by Yan Hui, Confucius's most talented disciple, when he said "with a deep sigh":

> The more I strain my gaze towards it the higher it soars. The deeper I bore down into it, the harder it becomes. I see it in front, but suddenly it is behind. Step by step, the master skilfully lures one on. He has broadened me with culture, restrained me with ritual. Even if I wanted to stop, I could not. Just when I feel that I have exhausted every resource, something seems to rise up, standing over me sharp and clear. Yet though I long to pursue it, I can find no way of getting to it at all.[35]

Ren took him beyond the confines of selfishness and gave him fleeting intimations of a sacred dimension that was both immanent and transcendent—welling up from within and yet also an accompanying presence, "standing over me sharp and clear."

Confucius died in 479 BCE, regarding himself as a failure because he had never been able to persuade a ruler to adopt a more compassionate policy. Yet he had made an indelible impression on Chinese spirituality; even those who disagreed with him would not be able to escape his influence. One of these was Mozi (c. 470–c. 391 BCE), who seems to have come from a humbler background and had little patience with the aristocratic *li.* By this time China had entered the terrible epoch known as the Warring States, in which the larger kingdoms systematically destroyed the small principalities and then fought one another until, when the conflict ended in 221, only one—the state of Qin—was left. Warfare itself had been transformed.[36] The old battle rituals cast aside, war was now conducted with deadly efficiency and enhanced technology, and was masterminded by military experts wholly intent on subjugating the population, even if this meant the death of women, children, and old men. It was a frightening warning of what could happen when the passions of the old brain were married to the new. Mozi's message was utilitarian and pragmatic. The thread that ran through his philosophy, like Confucius's, was *ren,* but he believed—wrongly—that Confucius had distorted the ethic by confining it to the family. He wanted to replace the potential egotism of kinship with a wider altruism: "Others must be regarded like the self," he insisted; this love must be "all embracing and exclude nobody."[37] The only way to prevent the Chinese from slaughtering one another was to persuade the rulers to practice *jian ai*.

Jian ai is often translated as "universal love," but this phrase is too emotive for the tough-minded Mozi.[38] A better translation is "concern for everybody"; *ai* was an impartial benevolence that had little to do with feeling but was based on a deep-rooted sense of equity and a disciplined respect for every single human being. Without this broader benevolence, even the positive virtues of family love and patriotism could degenerate into collective egotism. At present, Mozi argued, the rulers loved only their own states and felt no scruples about attacking others. But this would be impossible if they were taught to have as much concern for others as for themselves: "Regard another's state as you regard your own and another's person as you regard your own," he urged. "If the lords of the states are concerned for each other, they will not go to war." He was convinced that "in all cases, the reason why the world's calamities, dispossessions, resentments and hatreds arise is lack of *jian ai*."[39]

Mozi argued his position with a pragmatism that resonates with our own situation in the twenty-first century, asking rulers to weigh the cost of war against its benefits: warfare ruined harvests, killed thousands of civilians, and wasted expensive weapons and horses. The capture of a small town could result in unacceptably high casualties at a time when men were needed to farm the land. How could that be to the advantage of any state? The larger kingdoms thought that they would gain by conquering the smaller principalities, but in fact their wars benefited only a tiny portion of their people. Whereas if everybody could be persuaded to respect others as they did themselves, there would be peace and harmony throughout the world. If a ruler practiced *jian ai*, how could he raze a city to the ground or massacre the population of an entire village? And the good accruing from an impartial concern for everybody was incalculable:

> Now if we seek to benefit the world by taking *jian ai* as our standard, those with sharp ears and clear eyes will see and hear for others, those with sturdy limbs will work for others, and those with a knowledge of the Way will endeavour to teach others. Those who are old and without wives and children will find means of support and be able to live out their days; the young and orphaned who have no parents will find someone to care for them and look after their needs.[40]

During the Warring States period, Mozi was more widely revered than Confucius, because he spoke so pertinently to the terror of the time. But the Confucians responded to the growing crisis in their own way. In 260 BCE, the army of Qin conquered the state of Zhao, the birthplace of the great Confucian scholar Xunzi (c. 340–245 BCE), massacring four hundred thousand Zhao prisoners of war, who were buried alive. But Xunzi refused to lose faith. He still believed that the "yielding" spirit of the rituals could bring China back from the abyss, although he admitted that in these hard times they would have to be backed up with incentives and punishments. He remained convinced that a charismatic, compassionate ruler could save the world:

> He takes up arms in order to put an end to violence and to do away with harm, not in order to compete with others for spoil. Therefore when the soldiers of the benevolent man encamp, they command a god-like respect; and where they pass, they transform the people. They are like seasonable rain in whose falling all men rejoice.[41]

It was a beautiful vision, and although Xunzi had to admit that the Confucians had never succeeded in persuading rulers to let the Golden Rule guide their policies, he insisted that it was not an impossible ideal. Any man in the street, he believed, could become a Confucian sage.

The violence and cruelty of the Warring States had made Xunzi more acutely aware than Confucius of the darkness of the human heart. Everybody, he said, "is born with feelings of envy and hate, and if he indulges these, they will lead him into violence and crime, and all sense of loyalty and good faith will disappear."[42] But if he found a good teacher, submitted himself wholeheartedly to the *li* that taught him to treat others with respect, and obeyed the rules of society, he could become a sage.[43] It was no good doing what came naturally or relying on Heaven, the High God of China, to step in. It was pointless singing hymns to Heaven and paying no heed to the conduct of human affairs. If we concentrated on Heaven and neglected what human beings could do for themselves, Xunzi insisted again and again, "we fail to understand the nature of things."[44]

According to popular legend, the rituals (*li*) had been devised in remote antiquity by the legendary sage kings of China, Yao, Shun, and Yu. Xunzi argued that when these saintly men had contemplated the world, they realized that the only way they could end the intolerable misery they saw all around them was by a huge intellectual effort that began with the transformation of their own selves. So they created *li* based on *shu* ("likening to oneself") and the Golden Rule to moderate their own unruly passions, and when they put them into practice, they discovered an inner peace. By looking into their own hearts, critically observing their behavior, and taking note of their own reactions to pain and joy, these sages found a way to order social relations.[45] A ruler could bring peace and order to society only if he had mastered his own primitive instincts. The rituals, Xunzi believed, had been inspired by the sages' analysis of humanity; they had shaped the basic emotions engendered by our brain, just as an artist skillfully brought form and beauty out of unpromising material: they "trim what is too long, and stretch out what is too short, eliminate surplus and repair deficiency, extend the forms of love and reverence, and step by step, bring to fulfilment the beauties of proper conduct."[46] Even the stars, the planets, and the four seasons had to "yield" to one another to bring order out of potential chaos.[47] So far from being unnatural, the *li* would bring a practitioner into alliance with the way things are and into the heart of reality.

The three monotheistic religions also stressed the importance of compassion. Christianity and Rabbinic Judaism, the form of faith practiced by most Jews today, both developed during a period of warfare and economic exploitation. The Jewish uprising against the Roman occupation of Judaea resulted in the destruction of Jerusalem and its temple by the Roman army in 70 CE. Hitherto there had been no single Jewish orthodoxy; the period leading up to the catastrophe of 70 had been characterized by a rich religious diversity and a multitude of competing sects, all of which claimed to be the true Judaism and all preoccupied with the status and rituals of the temple. After the destruction of that temple, only two of these sects—the Jesus movement and Pharisaism—were able to survive.

Building on the insights of the Pharisees, the rabbis of the Talmudic age were able to transform Judaism from a temple faith into a religion of the book. Hitherto the study of the Torah (the teachings and laws attributed to Moses) had been a minority pursuit; now it would replace temple worship. In the course of a massively creative intellectual effort, the rabbis composed new scriptures: the Mishnah, completed in about 200 CE, and the Jerusalem and Babylonian Talmuds, completed in the fifth and sixth centuries respectively. Compassion was central to their vision, as we see in a famous story attributed to the great sage Hillel, an older contemporary of Jesus's. It is said that a pagan approached Hillel and promised to convert to Judaism if he could recite the entire Torah while he stood on one leg. Hillel replied: "What is hateful to yourself, do not to your fellow man. That is the whole of the Torah and the remainder is but commentary. Go study it."[48]

This provocative statement was intended to shock the audience into an appreciation of the importance of compassion. There is no mention of such doctrines as the unity of God, the creation of the world, the exodus from Egypt, or the 613 commandments. For Hillel, all these were simply a "commentary" on the Golden Rule. Other monotheists would come to the same conclusion. It is not that other devotions and beliefs are unimportant; the point is that there is something wrong with any spirituality that does not inspire selfless concern for others. Hillel was also making a statement about exegesis, the interpretation of scripture. He concludes with a *miqra*, a "call to action": "Go study!" As they scrutinized the ancient texts in an effort to make them speak to the post-temple age, Jews should use their creative insights to make them all a "commentary," a mere gloss, on the Golden Rule.

The great rabbi Akiva, executed by the Romans in 135 CE, taught that the commandment "Thou shalt love thy neighbor as thyself" was the greatest principle of the Torah.[49] Only his pupil Ben Azzai disagreed, preferring the simple biblical statement "This is the roll of the descendents of Adam" because it emphasized the unity of the human race.[50] In order to reveal the presence of compassion at the core of all the legislation and narratives of the Torah, the rabbis would sometimes twist the original sense and even change the words of scripture. They were not interested in merely elucidating the original intention of the biblical author. *Midrash* ("exegesis") was an essentially inventive discipline, deriving from the verb *darash,* "to search," "to investigate," or "to go in pursuit of" something that was not immediately self-evident. A rabbi would be expected to find fresh meaning in scripture, which, as the word of God, was infinite and could not be tied down to a single interpretation.

Another famous story shows that from the very beginning, the rabbis realized that compassion was the key to religion now that the temple had been destroyed.

> It happened that R. Johanan ben Zakkai went out from Jerusalem and R. Joshua followed him and saw the burnt ruins of the Temple and he said: "Woe is it that the place, where the sins of Israel find atonement, is laid waste." Then said R. Johanan, "Grieve not, we have an atonement equal to the Temple, the doing of loving deeds [*gemilut hasadim*], as it is said, 'I desire love [*hesed*] and not sacrifice.'"[51]

Practically expressed compassion was now a priestly act that would atone for sins more effectively than the temple sacrifices. It is a good example of the new midrash. Rabbi Johanan is quoting the prophet Hosea, who would probably have been surprised by his interpretation.[52] In its original context, *hesed* had meant not "love" but "loyalty"; for Hosea, God had not been speaking of the loving deeds that Jews would perform for one another but of the cultic fealty that Israelites owed to *him*.

The rabbis had seen too much of the horror of warfare

to condone the old chauvinisms. Not only had they witnessed the destruction of their holy city in 70, but the Bar
Kochba revolt against the Roman occupation in 132–35 CE
had resulted in catastrophic loss of Jewish life. Judaism,
like the other monotheisms, is not a wholly pacifist religion; warfare is permitted, but only in self-defense.[53] Yet
for the rabbis, peace (*shalom*) is one of the highest values of
all: *shalom* was more than a mere absence of conflict; it can
also be translated as "wholeness, completion." *Shalom* was
to be pursued as a positive harmonious principle in which
opposites could be reconciled.[54] The rabbis cited the Jewish
command "You shall not hate your brother in your heart,"
pointing out that it was not sufficient to refrain from curs-
ing or slapping your neighbor, but that enmity had to be
extirpated from the deepest reaches of the mind[55] and
that hatred of one's fellow creatures put a man beyond the
pale.[56] True power lay not in martial strength but in compassion and reconciliation. "Who is mighty?" the rabbis
asked. "He who turns an enemy into a friend."[57]

In their interpretation of the biblical doctrine of creation, the rabbis focused on the fact that all human beings
were made in God's image. To show disrespect to anyone
was therefore regarded as a denial of God himself and tan-
tamount to atheism, and murder was not simply a crime
against humanity but a sacrilege.[58] God had created only
one man at the beginning of time to teach us that destroying a single life was equivalent to annihilating the world,
while to save a life redeemed the entire human race.[59] To
humiliate anybody—even a slave or a non-Jew—was, like
murder, a sacrilegious desecration of God's image, and to

spread a libelous story about anybody at all was to deny God's existence.[60] Charity was the ultimate test of faith. You could not worship God unless you honored your fellow humans, whoever they might be.

Compassion seems also to have been central to the Christian ethos from the beginning. Like Hillel, Jesus taught the Golden Rule—but in its positive formulation.[61] Like the rabbis, he believed that the commandments to love God with your whole heart and soul and your neighbor as yourself were the most exalted commandments of the Torah.[62] The gospels show him practicing "concern for everybody," reaching out to "sinners": prostitutes, lepers, epileptics, and those denounced as traitors for collecting the Roman taxes. His followers should refrain from judging others.[63] The people admitted to the Kingdom of God, in which rich and poor would sit together at the same table, were those who practiced deeds of loving kindness, feeding the hungry and visiting those who were sick or in prison.[64] His most devoted disciples must give all their possessions to the poor.[65] Jesus is also presented as a man of *ahimsa*. "You have heard how it was said: *Eye for eye and tooth for tooth,*" he told the crowds. "But I say this to you: offer the wicked man no resistance. On the contrary, if anyone hits you on the right cheek, offer him the other as well."[66]

> You have heard how it was said; you must love your neighbour and hate your enemy. But I say this to you: love your enemies and pray for those who persecute you; in this way you will be sons of your father in heaven, for he causes his sun to rise on bad men as

well as good and his rain to fall on honest men alike. For if you love those who love you, how can you claim any credit? Even the tax-collectors and the pagans do as much, do they not? And if you save your greetings for your brothers, are you doing anything exceptional? You must be perfect, as your heavenly father is perfect.[67]

Like the rabbis, Jesus brought the compassionate message of scripture to the fore by giving a more stringently empathetic twist to an ancient text. Here he comes close to the Buddhist ideal of *upeksha,* "equanimity." His followers would offer kindness where there was little hope of any return.

Saint Paul, the earliest extant Christian writer, quoting an early Christian hymn, presents Jesus as a bodhisattva figure who refused to cling to the high status befitting one made in God's image and lived as the servant of suffering humanity.[68] Christians should do the same: "Everybody is to be self-effacing," Paul insisted. "Always consider the other person to be better than yourself, so that nobody thinks of his own interests first, but everybody thinks of other people's interests instead."[69] Compassion was the test of true spirituality:

If I have all the eloquence of men or of angels, but speak without love, I am simply a gong booming or a cymbal clashing. If I have the gift of prophecy, understanding all the mysteries there are, and knowing everything, and if I have faith in all its fullness, to move mountains, but without love, then I am nothing at all. If I give away all that I possess, piece by piece, and if I even let them take my body to burn it, but am without love, it will do me no good whatever.[70]

The earliest Christian community was remembered as a community of love, "united heart and soul"[71] and deliberately turning away from the me-first drive to acquire more and more: "The faithful all lived together and owned everything in common; they sold their goods and possessions and shared out the proceeds among themselves according to what each one needed."[72]

But that, of course, is not the whole story. There is a great deal of tribalism in both the Jewish and Christian scriptures. Hence we find texts such as the book of Joshua, which describes Israel's brutal slaughter of the indigenous people of Canaan, and the book of Revelation, which imagines Christ slaughtering his enemies in the Last Days. Not surprisingly, some have been puzzled by the Charter for Compassion's call "to return to the ancient principle that any interpretation of scripture that breeds violence, hatred or disdain is illegitimate."

But we have to remember that people have not always read scripture in the way it is read today. Rabbinic midrash was not interested in the original meaning of the biblical author; far from sticking slavishly to the literal sense of the ancient scriptures, the rabbis sought a radically new interpretation for a drastically altered world. They took from the old texts what was useful to them and set the rest reverently aside. Henceforth Jews would read the Hebrew Bible through the lens of the Mishnah and the Talmuds, which entirely transformed it. Christians were equally selective in their exegesis of the Hebrew Bible, focusing on texts that seemed to predict the coming of the Messiah (which they understood in an entirely different way) and paying little attention to the rest. Even Martin Luther (1483–1546), who saw scripture as the only valid path to God, found that he had to create a canon within the canon, because some biblical texts were more helpful than others. The reading of the Bible was, therefore, a highly selective process, and until the early modern period nobody thought of focusing solely on its literal meaning. Instead, Christians in Europe were taught to expound every sentence of the Bible in four ways: literally, morally, allegorically, and mystically. Indeed, as a Catholic child in the 1950s, this was how I was taught to read the Bible. For the Christians as for the rabbis, charity was the key to correct exegesis. Saint Augustine (354–430), one of the most formative theologians in the Western Christian tradition, insisted that scripture taught nothing but charity. Whatever the biblical author may have intended, any passage that seemed to preach hatred and was not conducive to love must be interpreted allegorically and made to speak of charity.[73]

In many ways, Islam can be seen as an inspired attempt to counter the violence of tribalism, urging Muslims to use their new-brain capacities to control and redirect their aggression. For centuries, Arabs had lived a desperate nomadic life in the inhospitable Arabian steppes, perpetually on the brink of starvation and malnutrition. Their chivalric code was called *muruwah*, which is difficult to translate succinctly; it meant courage and endurance, a determination to avenge any wrong done to the tribe, to protect its more vulnerable members, to respond instantly to any perceived threat, and to defy all enemies. Each tribesman had to be ready to leap to the defense of his kinfolk at a second's notice and to obey his chief unreservedly, right or wrong. "I am of Ghazziyya," sang one of the ancient poets. "If she be in error, I will be in error; and if Ghazziyya be guided right, I will go with her." Or as a popular maxim had it: "Help your brother whether he is being wronged or wronging others."[74] This loyalty, of course, extended only to your tribal unit: outsiders were regarded as worthless and expendable, and if you had to kill them to protect your fellow tribesmen, you wasted no time on regret.

Hence tribal existence was characterized by *jahiliyyah,* a word traditionally used to refer to the pre-Islamic period in Arabia and translated as "the Time of Ignorance." But though the root *JHL* has connotations of ignorance, its primary meaning was "irascibility." In the early Muslim texts, *jahiliyyah* denotes aggression, arrogance, chauvinism, and a chronic tendency toward violence and retaliation.[75] By the late sixth century CE, when the Prophet Muhammad was born, tribal warfare had reached an unprecedented level, and there was an apocalyptic sense of impending disaster.

The Quraysh, Muhammad's tribe, had left the nomadic life behind and established a commercial empire based in the city of Mecca. In order to make trade possible, they had abjured tribal warfare, cultivated an attitude of lofty neutrality toward local disputes, and made the area surrounding the Kabah, the ancient shrine in the middle of Mecca, a sanctuary in which violence was forbidden. These measures enabled Arabs from all over the peninsula to do business there without fear of vendetta. But the Quraysh had retained the old *jahili* arrogance. They had succeeded beyond their wildest dreams and were now free from the terror of want, but in their desire for wealth they had forgotten some of the more humane aspects of the tribal system. Instead of looking after weaker tribal members, some families were forging ahead and becoming richer, while others were impoverished and marginalized. There was resentment and spiritual malaise, since the old tribal rituals no longer spoke to the new conditions in their infant market economy. The Arabs knew about the God of the Jews and Christians and believed that he was identical with their own High God, *Allah,* a word that simply means "God," but were painfully aware that he had sent them no prophet and no scripture in their own language.

But that changed in 610, when Muhammad began to receive revelations that would eventually be collected in the scripture known as the Qur'an. These inspired oracles spoke directly to conditions in Mecca and articulated a compassionate ethos to counter its aggressive capitalism. The basic message of the Qur'an is that it is wrong to build a private fortune but good to share your wealth fairly to create a just and decent society where poor, vulnerable people are treated with respect. "Not one of you can be a believer," Muhammad said in an off-quoted maxim (*hadith*), "unless he desires for his neighbor what he desires for himself."

To replace the aggressive *jahili* ethos, the Qur'an proposed *hilm* ("mercy"), another traditional but less popular Arab virtue.[76] Men and women of *hilm* were forbearing, patient, and merciful; instead of venting their wrath, they would remain calm even in the most exasperating circumstances; they did not hit back when they suffered injury but were slow to retaliate, leaving revenge to Allah.[77] Those who practiced *hilm* looked after the poor, the disadvantaged, the orphan, and the widow, feeding the destitute even when they were hungry themselves.[78] They would behave always with consummate gentleness and courtesy. Men and women of peace, they "walk gently on the earth, and whenever the *jahilun* address them [insultingly], they reply 'Peace' [*salam*]."[79]

To counter the arrogant self-sufficiency of *jahiliyyah*, Muhammad asked his followers to make an existential "surrender" (*islam*) of their entire being to Allah, the Compassionate (*al-Rahman*) and Merciful (*al-Rahim*), who had given "signs" (*ayat*) of his benevolence to human beings in all the wonders of the created world.[80] A *muslim* was a man or woman who had made this surrender of ego. One of the first things Muhammad asked his converts to do was to prostrate themselves in prayer several times a day; it was difficult for Arabs imbued with the haughty *jahili* spirit to grovel on the ground like a slave, but the posture of their bodies was designed to teach them at a level deeper than the rational that the "surrender" of *islam* entailed daily transcendence of the preening, prancing ego. Muslims were also required to give a regular proportion of their income to the poor; this *zakat* ("purification") would purge their hearts of residual selfishness. At first the religion preached by Muhammad was called *tazakkah,* an obscure word related to *zakat,* which means "refinement, generosity, chivalry." Muslims were to cloak themselves in the virtues of compassion, using their intelligence to contemplate God's "signs" in nature in order to cultivate a similarly caring and responsible spirit that would make them want to give graciously to all God's creatures. Because of Allah's bountiful kindness, there was order and fertility where there could have been chaos and sterility. If they followed this example, they would find that instead of being trapped in the selfish barbarism of *jahiliyyah,* they would acquire spiritual refinement.

Islam is not a pacifist religion; Muhammad had to fight a war of self-defense against the Qurayshi establishment of Mecca, who had vowed to exterminate the Muslim community. Aggression and the preemptive strike were strictly forbidden. Sometimes fighting was necessary to preserve such humane values as religious freedom.[81] But it was always better to forgive and to sit down quietly and reason with your enemy, provided that this dialogue was conducted "in the most kindly manner."[82] Tragically, Muhammad found that war had its own deadly dynamic; in the desperate struggle, atrocities were committed by both sides. So as soon as the tide turned in his favor, Muhammad adopted a nonviolent policy, riding unarmed with a thousand unarmed Muslims into enemy territory. There, having narrowly escaped being massacred by the Meccan cavalry, he negotiated a treaty with the Quraysh, accepting terms that seemed to his outraged followers to throw away all the advantages they had gained. Yet that evening, the

Qur'an declared that this apparent defeat was a "manifest victory." While the Quraysh had behaved according to the violent *jahili* spirit, harboring "stubborn disdain in their hearts," God had sent down the "gift of inner peace" upon the Muslims, so that they had been able to respond to this assault with calm serenity.[83] The treaty that had seemed so unpromising led to a final peace: two years later, in 630, the Meccans voluntarily opened their gates to the Muslims.

It is important to comment on the traditional method of interpreting the Qur'an, which is an entirely different kind of scripture from the Bible. Instead of being a library of disparate texts composed over a millennium, the Qur'an was created in a mere twenty-three years and must be seen as a homogeneous whole. The word *qur'an* means "recitation." It is not designed to be read from cover to cover; instead, the words, chanted by a skilled reciter, are meant to be listened to. The sound of the words is an important part of their meaning. Themes, words, phrases, and sound patterns recur throughout the text, like variations on a piece of music, pulling widely separated parts of the scripture together so that over the years it forms a cohesive entity in the mind of the individual who spends a lifetime listening to evocative Qur'anic recitations. In the Qur'an, God told Muhammad, "Do not approach the Qur'an in haste, ere it has been revealed to thee in full."[84] On the basis of this text Muslims have traditionally been warned against a "hasty" approach, which draws hurried conclusions from isolated verses taken out of context. They should, rather, allow the whole scripture to take root in their minds before they attempt to interpret the details. Every single recitation of the Qur'an begins with an invocation to the mercy and compassion of God. And the relatively few texts dealing with the conduct of battle are counterbalanced by the far more numerous verses that speak of gentleness, forgiveness, kindness, courtesy, friendship, and forbearance.

Most readers will be more familiar with one of these traditions than with the others and at this point will want to explore its teachings in greater depth. But it is important, even at this very early stage in the twelve-step program, to become aware of the dynamic of other faiths too. Compassion requires us to open our hearts and minds to all others. As Mozi explained, we must have "concern for everybody," and, as the Buddha taught, we should make an effort to extend our benevolence to the farthest reaches of the world. This means that we must get to know about our neighbors in the global village and realize that our own tradition is not alone in its pursuit of the compassionate ideal. The comparative study of other religions is not designed to dilute your appreciation of your own or to make you convert to another tradition. Ideally it should help you to see the faith that you are most familiar with in a different, richer light. Each of the world religions has its own particular genius, its own special insight into the nature and requirements of compassion, and has something unique to teach us. By making room in your mind for other traditions, you are beginning to appreciate what many human beings, whatever their culture and beliefs, hold in common. So while you are investigating the teachings of your own tradition, take time to find out more about the way other faiths have expressed the compassionate ethos. You will find that this in itself will enable you to expand your sympathies and begin to challenge some of the preconceptions that separate us from "the other."

But as we begin our journey, we should recall that the sages, prophets, and mystics of these traditions did not regard compassion as an impractical dream. They worked as hard to implement it in the difficult circumstances of their time as we work today to find a cure for cancer. They were innovative thinkers, ready to use whatever tools lay to hand in order to reorient the human mind, assuage suffering, and pull their societies back from the brink. They did not cynically throw up their hands in despair, but insisted that every person had the ability to reform himself or herself and become an icon of kindness and selfless empathy in a world that seemed ruthlessly self-destructive. We need that energy and conviction today.

THE SECOND STEP

Look at Your Own World

It was important to begin by considering the ideas of some of the great luminaries of the past. As we have seen, they adapted the insights of the primordial faith traditions, which had always understood the value of compassion, to the requirements of a dramatically changed world—an urbanized society; large, industrializing states; escalating violence; and an aggressive commercial economy. They did not feel that religion mired them in the past but were ready to make fundamental changes in the traditions they had inherited: we need only think of the Buddha, going from one guru to another in search of enlightenment before deciding to go his own way. We also have the example of the rabbis, who were ready even to change the words of the Bible in order to address the current problems of the community. Finally, we should consider the heroism of

Muhammad, whose plan to create a community based on a shared ideology rather than the sacred tie of blood was a radical break with the past. As we seek to create a more compassionate world, we too must think outside the box, reconsider the major categories of our time, and find new ways of dealing with today's challenges.

But as we approach this task, we need the guidance of such people as the Buddha or Confucius, because they are the experts. In the West, our achievements have been scientific and technological, and we have had few spiritual geniuses. Our scientific focus on the external world has been of immense benefit to humanity, but we are less adept in the exploration of the interior life. We have been unable spiritually to go beyond the paradigmatic insights of the great sages of the past. But we have also seen that many of these pivotal teachers and prophets were living in societies that had problems similar to our own: they were dealing with violence that seemed to be getting out of hand and an economy that marginalized the poor. All were disturbed by the spectacle of ubiquitous suffering. It is now time to apply what we have learned from them to our own circumstances and to the society in which we live.

Joseph Campbell has shown that every single culture developed its own myth of the hero, an outstanding individual who transformed the life of his people at immense cost to himself. The story always takes the same basic form so must express a universal insight.[1] In all these tales, the hero begins by looking around his society and finding that something is missing. Perhaps there is spiritual malaise;

perhaps traditional ideas no longer speak to his contemporaries; perhaps they are facing some unusual danger. He can find no ready-made solution, so he decides to leave home, turn his back on everything safe and familiar, and find a different answer. His quest is heroic because it demands self-sacrifice: the hero will experience pain, rejection, isolation, danger, and even death. But he is willing to undertake this journey out of love for his people—a devotion that does not consist of wordy declarations but of practically expressed altruism. The purpose of this myth is to help us to unleash our own heroic potential, to show us what we must do if we want to create a better world and how best to meet the challenges of our time.

Many of the biographies of the great religious leaders follow this pattern. The Buddha had to leave the comforts of home, abandon his weeping parents, shave his head, and don the yellow robes of a world-renouncing ascetic when he set out to find a cure for the world's pain.[2] At the start of his career, Jesus was "led by the Spirit" into the desert, a place of transformation in biblical lore but also the haunt of demons: he is taken to the pinnacle of the temple and up a high mountain to survey the world from a detached vantage point, where he assesses and rejects the allure of an easier, showier, and more obvious path.[3] Long before he received any revelations, every year Muhammad used to retreat to Mount Hira just outside Mecca. Here he fasted, performed spiritual exercises, and gave alms to the poor while he meditated on the creeping malaise that was overtaking his fellow tribesmen, searching intently for a remedy. Many of the more recent heroes of compassion have undergone the same process. When he returned to India from South Africa, for example, Gandhi left the city elites behind and traveled all over the country, carefully observing the plight of the ordinary people, before deciding on a course of action.

So during this step, we should take ourselves mentally to the summit of a high mountain, where can stand back and see things from a different perspective. As you undertake this exercise, it might be helpful to think in terms of the Confucian concentric circles of compassion, starting with your family, moving out to your friends and community, and finally to the country in which you live. Many of the things we have long taken for granted—our financial institutions and our political policies, both at home and abroad—seem suddenly inadequate. We are unable to deal with the massive problems of hunger and poverty; we know that our environmental policies are unsustainable, and yet we cannot seem to find a viable way of dealing with them. We look around us and realize that something needs to be done, yet find no immediate solutions. But we should not approach our task with the harsh zeal of a reformer; there should be no anger, frustration, or impatience in our survey. We must look at our community with compassion, estimate its strengths as well as its weaknesses, and assess its potential for change.

Let us start with the family. It is true, as the old adage says, that charity begins at home. As the Confucians have taught us, the family is a school of compassion because it is here that we learn to live with other people. Family life

involves self-sacrifice, because daily we have to put ourselves to one side in order to accommodate the needs of
other family members; nearly every day there is something
to forgive. Instead of seeing this as an irritant, we should
see these tensions as opportunities for growth and transformation. Ask yourself what you really feel about your
family. What makes you proud and happy about them?
Make a list of the ways in which your family nourishes you.
Perhaps you could write a letter to them outlining your
history as a family, and your hopes and fears for each person in it. Does your family have a black sheep, and how
has this situation come about? Can it be rectified? How do
you conduct arguments and disagreements? What are your
particular strengths in family life? Is there anything more
you could do?

The Confucians believed in the importance of ritual
in family life. In ancient China, each family member had
to subordinate his or her needs to another: the older son
to his parents, a wife to her husband, and a younger son to
his older brother. The system was so designed that there
was an interchange of reverence and everybody received
a measure of respect. The older son, for example, would
probably become a parent himself and be served by his son
in the same manner as he was serving his own father. You
might have both an older and a younger brother, so you
were nourished by the rituals of consideration at the same
time as you were bestowing them. The *li* required a son to
submit absolutely to his father's wishes, but the father was
supposed to behave fairly, kindly, and courteously to his
children. Family life was seen as similar to the carefully

choreographed ritual ballets of ancient China, a series of interweaving and reciprocal dances in which each person had a partner and contributed to the beauty of the whole. The *li* gave all family members training in empathy: when his father died, for example, the eldest son would withdraw from the family home and fast, sharing his father's growing weakness and suspension between life and death.

None of this, of course, will do today. In the West, for example, we value the independence of the young, expect them to speak their minds, and do not exact absolute obedience. But are we treating the elderly members of the family with an empathetic love and respect? Do they die surrounded with care, or are they shunted into impersonal nursing homes and hospices? If they are at home, are they treated only with perfunctory consideration and regarded as a burden? Are some people carrying more than their share of the responsibility of care? Confucius was incensed to see that instead of making their parents' meals an elegant, gracious ceremony, many sons were simply throwing the food in front of them. "Even dogs and horses are cared for to that extent!" Confucius exclaimed.[4] "Filial piety does not consist merely in young people undertaking the hard work when anything has to be done," he insisted; "it is something more than that." This elusive "something" was the "demeanor": you revealed the spirit in which you were carrying out these rites of service in every one of your gestures and facial expressions.[5] The care of the elderly is going to be a big problem in those Western countries with an increasingly aged population. Can we learn something about the compassionate care of the elderly from Confucius?

Can you think of a twenty-first-century equivalent to the *li* that would make each member of the family feel supremely valued? How can you make your family a school for compassion, where children learn the value of treating all others with respect? What would life be like if all family members made a serious attempt to treat one another "all day and every day" as they would wish to be treated themselves? How would life be improved, for example, if everybody made a consistent effort to avoid speaking too hastily? We know that people brought up in dysfunctional families find it difficult to make good relationships in later life; they can have psychological problems that cause them to increase the sum of pain in the world. Creating a compassionate family life is one of the ways in which we can all make a constructive contribution to a more empathetic society in the future.

Next, we should consider the workplace. How can a lawyer, businessperson, construction worker, doctor, educator, clergyperson, dog walker, police officer, traffic warden, nurse, shop assistant, caregiver, librarian, chef, cab driver, receptionist, author, secretary, cleaner, or banker observe the Golden Rule in the course of his or her work? What would be the realistic criteria of a compassionate company? If your profession made a serious attempt to become more compassionate, what impact would this have on your immediate environment and the global community? To whom in your profession and your own place of work would you give a Golden Rule prize? We are target-driven in modern society, often geared for efficiency rather than compassion. Do we treat colleagues and workers as cogs in the wheel, forcing them to maximize output at the expense of their physical, mental, and spiritual health? Does the need to create a competitive edge endorse and aggravate the me-first drive that makes us heartless in other areas of life? The acquisitive drive of the reptilian brain evolved for scarcity, not plenty. Do we find it difficult to say "enough"?

Finally, we should take a dispassionate look at our nation. First, ask yourself what it is that you love most about your country. What has your nation done for the world in the past, and what can it realistically do to make the world a more just, fair, safe, and peaceful place? Most of us believe that our nation has compassionate values, but can you imagine what it would be like if it became *more* compassionate? How would this affect the global community? And what would a compassionate modern nation-state be like? What would be the minimum requirements for a compassionate modern state? And how can a modern politician observe the Golden Rule in his or her domestic and foreign policy?

In political life, Confucius explained, if we seek to establish ourselves, we should seek also to establish others; if we wish status and success for ourselves, we should make sure that others have it too; if we wish to turn our merits to account, we should make sure that others have the same opportunity. Has your nation been guilty of oppressing or even destroying other peoples in the past or in the present? How compassionate are its penal and social systems, its health care and environmental policies? Are its financial institutions guilty of me-first greed? How does your nation treat immigrants and ethnic minorities? Is there gross inequality between rich and poor? Is tribalism rife in your society? Are there signs of aggressive territorialism, hostility to rivals, contempt for outsiders, and fear of invaders? Is there a compulsion to belong, conform, and follow leaders uncritically?

It is crucial to educate the young in the compassionate ethos. Are the children of your nation encouraged to relate with respect to their peers, their teachers, and foreigners? What do their textbooks teach them about other races and peoples? Are students taught enough about the history of the nation so that they understand its flaws as well as its triumphs? Are there problems of drinking, drugs, violence, and bullying in your schools? Once you have considered these questions, if you are an educator, why not develop a curriculum to educate children in the importance of empathy and respect? If you work in technology, perhaps you could create a computer game that would accustom children to putting themselves into the shoes of a victim of bullying, a homeless person, a refugee, a new immigrant, an impoverished family, a person with physical or mental challenges, or a racially ostracized individual.

If you have formed a reading discussion group, you might like to discuss some of these issues. No single individual can take on all these problems. During this step, ask yourself what your particular contribution should be and where you should concentrate your efforts—in business, medicine, the media, education, the arts, politics, or in the home. Do not be overwhelmed by the immensity of the task ahead, because it is possible to change attitudes. In the 1960s, for example, civil rights activists and feminists transformed the way we speak and think about race and gender. Remember Xunzi's optimism and make it your own: every man or woman in the street can become a force for good in the world.

Compassion for Yourself

The late rabbi Albert Friedlander once impressed upon me the importance of the biblical commandment "Love your neighbor as yourself."[1] I had always concentrated on the first part of that injunction, but Albert taught me that if you cannot love yourself, you cannot love other people either. He had grown up in Nazi Germany, and as a child was bewildered and distressed by the vicious anti-Semitic propaganda that assailed him on all sides. One night, when he was about eight years old, he deliberately lay awake and made a list of all his good qualities. He told himself firmly that he was *not* what the Nazis said, that he had talents and special gifts of heart and mind, which he enumerated to himself one by one. Finally, he vowed that if he survived, he would use those qualities to build a better world. This was an extraordinary insight for a child in such circumstances. Albert was one of the kindest people I have ever met; he was almost pathologically gentle and must have brought help and counsel to thousands. But he always said that he could have done no good at all unless he had learned, at that terrible moment of history, to love himself.

We have seen that compassion is essential to humanity. We have a biological need to be cared for and to care for others. Yet it is not easy to love ourselves. In our target-driven, capitalist Western societies, we are more inclined to castigate ourselves for our shortcomings and become inordinately cast down by any failure to achieve our objectives and potential. It is a terrible irony that while many in the world are suffering from malnourishment and starvation, in the West an alarming number of women—and, increasingly, men—are afflicted with eating disorders that spring from a complex amalgam of self-hatred, fear, feelings of failure, inadequacy, helplessness, and yearning for control.[2] But this self-dissatisfaction is not confined to the West. In countries that were colonized by Europeans during the late nineteenth century, for example, people often internalized the colonialists' negative assessment of themselves. Muhammad Abdu (1849–1905), who would become Grand Mufti of Egypt, described the corrosive sense of inferiority that had crept into the lives of the colonized:

It is an age which has formed a bond between ourselves and the civilized nations, making us aware of their excellent conditions . . . and our mediocre situation: thus revealing their wealth and our poverty, their pride and our degradation, their strength and our weakness, their triumphs and our defects.[3]

Colonialism did not end when the colonialists returned home. On both sides, old attitudes have often persisted; the inferiority engendered in some sectors of the former colonies has festered and may lie at the root of some of our current political problems.

The Golden Rule requires self-knowledge; it asks that we use our own feelings as a guide to our behavior with others. If we treat ourselves harshly, this is the way we are likely to treat other people. So we need to acquire a healthier and more balanced knowledge of our strengths as well as our weaknesses. As we work through this step, we should all do what Rabbi Friedlander did that night and make a list of our good qualities, talents, and achievements. We recognize flaws in some of our closest friends, but this does not diminish our affection for them. Nor should it affect the way we value ourselves. Before we can make friends with others, we have to make a friend of our own self. Without denying your faults, remember all the people you have helped, the kind things you have done that nobody noticed, and your successes at home and at work. A sense of humor is also important: we should be able to smile wryly but gently at our failings, in the same way as we tease a friend.

It is essential to be aware of our misdeeds and take responsibility for them. But we should also realize that the rage, fear, hatred, and greed that make us behave badly derive from the brain we inherited from our reptilian ancestors. It is useless to castigate ourselves bitterly for feeling jealousy, anger, and contempt, as that will only lead to self-hatred. Instead, we should quietly but firmly refuse to identify with them, saying with the Buddha: "This is not mine; this is not what I really am; this is not my self."[4] It will not be easy, because the emotions of the old brain are powerful and automatic, but we can learn to distance ourselves from them by the practice of mindfulness, which we shall discuss when we come to the fifth step.

Fear is fundamental to the reptilian brain; it inspires two of the Four Fs, making us flee from or fight anything that threatens us. Fear makes us hate those we regard as dangerous. It makes us wary and suspicious: instead of reaching out to others, we shrink back into ourselves, warding off the impending menace. When we feel that our backs are to the wall, we may hit out violently. Everybody is afraid of something. What fills you with dread? Spiders, loneliness, cancer, death, a demented old age, failure, or poverty? Instead of despising yourself for these anxieties and castigating yourself for cowardice, be compassionate toward yourself and remember that fear is a human characteristic. It is something that links us with other people. If we cannot accept the reality of our own terror, we are likely to dismiss and even ridicule the fears of others. During the forthcoming steps, we will try to open our minds and hearts to people we find hostile and frightening. This takes courage, but it is the best way of overcoming our phobias. Remember how the sages of the Upanishads discovered that they became free of fear as a result of adopting a compassionate lifestyle and a mind-training regimen.

Some of our character traits are the result of circumstances beyond our control. So much of life is a given. We did not choose our parents, the genes we inherited, or the upbringing and education we received. We were not able to select the economic circumstances or the society into which we were born. We have to work hard to mitigate any ill effects of the environmental factors that have affected our personalities, but we should not assume that they have made us incapable of compassion. If we do that, we are likely to dismiss other people for their apparent inadequacies instead of reflecting that they did not choose their circumstances, parentage, or genetic makeup either.

It is important, however, to recognize that we all have a dark side. The Jungian psychologists speak of the "shadow," a mechanism that enables us to disguise from our conscious, waking selves the less savory motives, desires, and inclinations that influence our thoughts and behavior and sometimes surface in dreams. We need to take ownership of this nether region of the psyche so that we are not overwhelmed with horror if we discover that we are fascinated by cruelty, have strange sexual fantasies, or are suddenly consumed by the desire for violent retaliation. If we are unable to accept our shadow, we are likely to take a harsh view of the darker side of others. When people inveigh furiously against sexual depravity, violence, or cruelty, this can be a sign that they have failed to come to terms with their own proclivities and believe that it is only *other* people who are evil and disgusting.

We often attack other people for precisely those qualities that we most dislike in ourselves. This can lead us to project our less-than-admirable traits onto other people—a mechanism that has been responsible for much of the stereotypical thinking that has led to atrocity and persecution in the past. During the Middle Ages, for example, Christians evolved a belief in what is known as the "blood libel," claiming that Jews murdered little children and used their blood in the unleavened bread they ate at Passover; this terrifying image of the Jew as child slayer revealed an almost oedipal fear of the parent faith.[5] In a similar fashion, when the Crusaders slaughtered Muslims, they claimed that Islam was a violent religion of the sword—a fantasy with little basis in fact but that reflected buried anxiety and guilt about their own behavior. Jesus had, after all, told his followers to love their enemies, not to exterminate them. At a time when the papacy was trying to impose celibacy on the reluctant clergy, medieval Christians condemned Islam as a faith that encouraged Muslims to pander to their basest instincts.[6] In many ways, the Crusaders' attitude toward the Islamic world, which was far more powerful and sophisticated than Western Europe at this time, resembled the response of a modern Third World country to a great power. Their distorted view of Muslims was a compensation for their own feelings of inferiority. In their mingled fear, resentment, and envy, medieval Christians projected doubts about their own identity onto the Muslim foe. Islam had become the shadow self of Europe, a confused image of everything the Crusaders believed they were *not*—but feared that they *were*.

Suffering is a law of life, and it is essential during this step to acknowledge our own pain or we shall find it impossible to have compassion for the distress of others. In Buddhism, compassion (*karuna*) is defined as a determination to liberate others from their grief, something that is impossible if we do not admit to our own unhappiness and misery. Today in the West we are often encouraged to think positively, brace up, stiffen our upper lip, and look determinedly on the bright side of life. It is, of course, important to encourage the positive, but it is also crucial sometimes to allow ourselves to mourn. The ancient Greeks had no problem with shedding tears; they believed that weeping together created a bond between human beings. In Shakespeare's day it was considered quite normal for men to weep. Not anymore. Today there is often a degree of heartlessness in our determined good cheer, because if we simply tell people to be "positive" when they speak to us of their sorrow, we may leave them feeling misunderstood and isolated in their distress. Somebody once told me that when she had cancer, the hardest thing of all was her friends' relentless insistence that she adopt a positive attitude; they refused to let her discuss her fears—probably because they were frightened by her disease and found it an uncomfortable reminder of their own mortality.

When we contemplate the suffering we see on a global scale, we may be embarrassed by the triviality of our own. But it is real to us nonetheless. During this step, make a conscious effort to look back on the events that have caused you distress in the past: the death of a beloved person; moments of loneliness and abject fear; rejections, betrayals, and failures; the unkind remark that hurt you. Make a deliberate effort to inhabit those moments fully and send a message of encouragement and sympathy to your former self. The object of this exercise is not to leave you wallowing in self-pity. The vivid memory of painful times past is a reservoir on which you can draw when you try to live according to the Golden Rule. By remembering your own sorrow vividly, you will make it possible for yourself to feel empathy with others.

It is often tempting to envy those who lead apparently charmed lives. But even the most fortunate people will face death, sickness, and the possibility of a debilitating and humiliating old age. We know that nothing lasts; everything is impermanent, even our most intense moments of joy. That is why the Buddhists insist that existence is suffering (*dukkha*). A better translation would be "existence is awry." There is something wrong, incomplete, or unsatisfactory in almost any situation. If I get a wonderful job, the other candidates are disappointed. The beautiful shirt I have just bought may have been made in a sweatshop with appalling conditions for workers. In the course of a single day, we can be momentarily cast down by myriad tiny disappointments, rejections, frustrations, and failures. We are subject to minor physical distress, anxiety about our health, and fatigue. "Pain, grief and despair are *dukkha*," the Buddha explained. "Being forced into proximity with what we hate is suffering; being separated from what we love is suffering, not getting what we want is suffering."[7] Making ourselves aware of these small discomforts and the reality of our own *dukkha* is an essential step toward enlightenment and compassion.

We are so often the cause of our own misery. We pursue things and people even though we know in our heart of hearts that they cannot make us happy. We imagine that all our problems will be solved if we get a particular job or achieve a certain success—only to find that the things we desired so intensely are not so wonderful after all. The moment we acquire something, we start to worry about losing it. Much of our suffering comes from a thwarted sense of self. When we wake in the early hours of the morning, we toss and turn, asking: Why does nobody appreciate me? Why can I not have what X has? When we love people, we may become possessive and unreasonably angry if they declare independence of us. When we hear of somebody else's success, our first reaction is often a pang of jealousy or resentment. We feel impaired by a colleague's beauty or brilliance, waste an inordinate amount of energy worrying about our image and status, and are constantly alert to anything that might threaten our standing and self-esteem. We identify so closely with our opinions that we become disproportionately upset if we lose an argument. We are so anxious to see ourselves in a good light that we find it difficult to apologize wholeheartedly, often emphasizing that the other person was also at fault. The result of all this self-preoccupation is that we not only make ourselves suffer but we also cause pain to other people.

Instead of reviling ourselves for our chronic pettiness and selfishness, it is better to accept calmly the fact that the cause of such behavior is our old brain. Geared for survival, the reptilian brain was all about me. Without this ruthless self-preoccupation, our species would not have survived. Yet if we allow it to dominate our lives, we will be miserable and do our best to make other people unhappy. Our egotism gravely limits our view of the world, which we see through the distorting screen of our personal desires and needs. When we hear a piece of news, we immediately wonder how it will affect our own plans and prospects. When we meet somebody new, our first impressions are often colored by such speculations as: Am I attracted to her? Is he a threat? Can I use her in some way? As a result, we rarely see things or people as they are. We are frightened, insecure, and restless creatures, endlessly distressed by our failures and shortcomings, constantly poised against attack, and this can make us hostile and unkind to others.

During this step, we begin to practice the Buddha's meditation on the four immeasurable minds of love, which will be a central part of the program. There is no need to sit in a yogic position to meditate, unless you find it helpful to do so. This meditation can fit easily into your regular routine and be performed while you are walking the dog, exercising, driving the car, or gazing out of the window of your commuter train. The purpose of meditation is not to make contact with a god or a supernatural being; rather, it is a discipline that helps us to take greater control of our minds and channel our destructive impulses creatively.

You will recall that while he was working toward enlightenment, the Buddha devised a meditation that made him conscious of the positive emotions of friendship (*maitri*), compassion (*karuna*), joy (*mudita*), and "even-mindedness" (*upeksha*) that lay dormant in his mind. He then directed this "immeasurable" love to the ends of the earth. Later he would tell his monks to do the same:

> When your mind is filled with love, send it in one direction, then a second, a third, and a fourth, then above, then below. Identify with everything without hatred, resentment, anger or enmity. This mind of love is very wide. It grows immeasurably and eventually is able to embrace the whole world.[8]

Over time, the Buddha found that by constantly activating these positive psychological states he became free of the constrictions of hostility and fear, and that his own mind expanded with the immeasurable power of love.

But before you are ready to "embrace the whole world," you must focus on yourself. Begin by drawing on the warmth of friendship (*maitri*) that you know exists potentially in your mind and direct it to yourself. Notice how much peace, happiness, and benevolence you possess already. Make yourself aware of how much you need and long for loving friendship. Next, become conscious of your anger, fear, and anxiety. Look deeply into the seeds of rage within yourself. Bring to mind some of your past suffering. You long to be free of this pain, so try gently to put aside your current irritations, frustrations, and worries and feel compassion (*karuna*) for your conflicted, struggling self. Then bring your capacity for joy (*mudita*) to the surface and take conscious pleasure in things we all tend to take for granted: good health, family, friends, work, and life's tiny pleasures. Finally, look at yourself with *upeksha* ("even-mindedness, nonattachment"). You are not unique. You have failings, but so does everybody else. You also have talents and, like every other being on the planet, you deserve compassion, joy, and friendship.

It is only in the context of a kinder attitude toward ourselves that we can consider the importance of transcending the ego. The religions often speak of putting the self to death; Buddhists believe that the self is an illusion and teach a doctrine of "no-self" (*anatta*). Modern neuroscientists would agree: they can find nothing in the intricate activity of the brain that they can pin down and call a "self" or a "soul." But *anatta* is primarily a mythos calling Buddhists to action: we have to live *as though* the self did not exist, cutting through the self-obsession that causes so much pain. When the masters of the spiritual life ask us to transcend the ego, they want us to get beyond the grasping, frightened, angry self that often seeks to destroy others in order to ensure its own survival, prosperity, and success. This is indispensable to enlightenment. When the Dalai Lama called for a spiritual revolution on the eve of the third millennium, he explained that this did not mean embracing a particular religious creed. Rather, it would be based on a "radical reorientation away from our habitual preoccupation with self."[9]

This does not mean that we should recoil from ourselves with disgust, put ourselves down at every turn, and become hyperconscious of our faults. If we do this, there is a danger that we will simply become excessively self-conscious, mired in the insecure ego we are trying to transcend. The faith traditions agree that compassion is the most reliable way of putting the self in its proper place, because it requires us "all day and every day" to dethrone ourselves from the center of our world and put another there. As the Dalai Lama made plain, the reorientation away from self is essentially "a call to turn toward the wider community of beings with whom we are connected, and for conduct which recognizes others' interests alongside our own."[10] Compassion, he said, was impossible without self-restraint, because "we cannot be loving and compassionate unless at the same time we curb our own harmful impulses and desires."[11] Saint Paul made the same point: the practice of charity is incompatible with the hurtful stratagems we devise to undermine others and inflate the ego:

Love is always patient and kind; it is never jealous; love is never boastful or conceited; it is never rude or selfish; it does not take offence, and is not resentful. Love takes no pleasure in other people's wrongdoing but delights in truth; it is always ready to excuse, to trust, to hope, and to endure whatever comes.[12]

It takes courage to set the self aside. The Buddha knew that when somebody heard about *anatta* he was likely to panic, thinking: "I am going to be annihilated and destroyed; I will no longer exist."[13] Yet when his disciples were introduced to this doctrine, the texts tell us that their hearts were filled with joy.[14] As soon as they started to live as though the self were nonexistent, they felt happier, freed of the *dukkha* that comes from excessive self-preoccupation.

If we remain trapped in this greedy, needy selfishness, we will continue to be unhappy and frustrated. But as we acquire a more realistic assessment of ourselves, we learn that the envy, anger, fear, and hatred (which often spring from thwarted egotism) have little to do with us; rather, they are ancient emotions that we inherited from our earliest ancestors. "This is not what I really am," said the Buddha; "this is not my self." Gradually we will begin to feel more detached from these negative emotions and refuse to identify with them. We will also slowly become aware that our feelings about other people are often relative and subjective, bearing little relation to reality. Instead of being objective, rational assessments of others, they can simply be "all about me." As long as we allow them to dominate us, they will imprison us in a defensive, self-obsessed worldview, so that we never realize our full potential. A more productive way to deal with hostile feelings toward others is to realize that those we dislike are suffering from them in much the same way. When people attack us, they are probably experiencing a similar self-driven anxiety and frustration; they too are in pain. In time, if we persevere, the people we fear or envy become less threatening, because the self that we are so anxious to protect and promote at their expense is a fantasy that is making us petty and smaller than we need to be.

So when we make a conscious effort to abandon the me-first mentality and try to keep it within due bounds, we are not destroying or annihilating ourselves. Instead we will find that our horizons expand, our egotistically driven fears evaporate, and that we are experiencing a larger "immeasurable" self. Free of self-destructive emotion, we too can become a *junzi*, a fulfilled and mature human being. The rabbis discovered that when a Jew studied the Torah for its own sake rather than for personal gain, he was filled with a love that lifted him to a higher level of being. "He is called the Beloved Companion," said the great Talmudic sage Rabbi Meir. "He loves the Divine Presence and loves all creatures. . . . And he becomes like an overflowing fountain or a ceaseless torrent. . . . And it makes him great and lifts him above the entire creation."[15] The early Christians spoke of a new freedom when, like Jesus, they became sons of God; by emptying themselves of egotism, as Jesus did, they had intimations of his exalted state.[16] After emerging from their symbolic death in the baptismal pool, they were told that they too had become *christoi*.[17] The Greek Orthodox still maintain that we can be deified like the man Jesus even in this life.[18] The Confucians claimed that a life of *ren* expanded our humanity: "Broad and vast—who knows the limits of such a man?" asked Xunzi. "Brilliant and comprehensive—who knows his virtue? Shadowy and ever-changing—who knows his form? His brightness matches the sun and moon; his greatness fills the eight directions. Such is the Great Man."[19]

This was how his contemporaries saw the Buddha. One day a Brahmin priest found him sitting meditating under a tree and was astonished by his strength, serenity, and composure. "Are you a god, sir?" he asked. "Are you an angel . . . or a spirit?" No, the Buddha replied. The self that had held him in thrall had been "extinguished" by the cultivation of compassion, revealing a new potential in human nature by activating parts of his being that normally lay dormant. "Remember me," he told the priest, "as one who is awake."[20] A skeptic will dismiss these claims as delusory. But the only way to prove or disprove them is to put the method to the test. During the twelve steps, we are trying to awaken our potential for compassion, sagehood, and Buddhahood. Do not leave this step until you have laid the foundations for a healthy, realistic assessment of yourself and made the meditation on love a regular part of your day. Once you have started to feel a genuine compassion for yourself, you will be able to extend it to others.

Empathy

When the Buddha was born, his father invited the local priests to his home to tell the child's fortune. One of them predicted that he was destined to see three disturbing sights, which would inspire him to renounce the world and become a monk. The Buddha's father had more worldly ambitions for his son, so he immured the boy in a luxurious palace and posted guards around the grounds to keep all distressing reality at bay. It is a striking image of the mind in denial. As long as we close our minds to the pain that presses in upon us on all sides, we remain imprisoned in delusion, because this artificial existence bears no relation to reality. It is also futile, because suffering is inescapable and will always break through our carefully constructed defenses. When the Buddha was twenty-nine years old, the gods decided that he had lived in this fool's paradise long enough, so they sent four of their number past the guards into the grounds, disguised as a sick man, an old man, a corpse, and a monk. Utterly unprepared for these spectacles of suffering, the future Buddha was so shocked that he left home that very night determined to find a way to help himself and others to bear the sorrow of life with serenity, creativity, and kindness.

This story is a *mythos,* devised to show Buddhists what they had to do to achieve their own enlightenment. We cannot even begin our quest until we allow the ubiquitous *dukkha* of life to invade our minds and hearts. That is why nearly all the religious traditions put suffering at the top of their agenda. We would rather push it away and pretend that the ubiquitous grief of the world has nothing to do with us, but if we do that we will remain confined in an inferior version of ourselves. The definitive icon of Western Christianity is the image of a crucified man in an extremity of agony. It is an emblem of the cruelty that human beings have inflicted on one another from time immemorial. But it is also a pain that redeems the world. The Western Christian doctrine of atonement—one not held by the Greek Orthodox—is sometimes difficult to understand: it is hard to imagine how a compassionate God would demand such suffering as the price of our salvation. But the French philosopher Peter Abelard (c. 1079–1142) suggested an alternative: when we look at the crucifix, our hearts break in sympathy and fellow feeling—and it is this interior movement of compassion and instinctive empathy that saves us.

The ancient Greeks, founders of the Western rational

tradition, had a uniquely tragic view of life. Each year on the festival of Dionysus, god of transformation, the leading playwrights of Athens presented tragic trilogies in a drama competition, which every citizen was obliged to attend. The plays usually dramatized one of the old myths adapted to reflect the problems and situation of the city that year. This event was both a spiritual exercise and a civic meditation, which put suffering onstage and compelled the audience to empathize with men and women struggling with impossible decisions and facing up to the disastrous consequences of their actions. The Greeks came to the plays in order to weep together, convinced that the sharing of grief strengthened the bond of citizenship and reminded each member of the audience that he was not alone in his personal sorrow.

In his trilogy *Oresteia*, Aeschylus (525–456 BCE) showed that suffering was not only built into human experience but indispensable to the quest for wisdom. The three tragedies depict a seemingly unstoppable cycle of revenge killing. In the first play, Clytemnestra murders her husband, King Agamemnon, to avenge the death of their daughter; then the saga continues with the story of their son, Orestes, who slays his mother to avenge his father; the trilogy concludes with Orestes' headlong flight from the Erinyes (also known as the Furies), the terrifying gods of the underworld who would hound a transgressor like a pack of wild dogs until he atoned for his sin with a horrible death. Suffering was a law of life, the chorus reminds the audience, but it was also the path to wisdom:

Zeus has led us on to know,
the Helmsman lays it down as law
that we must suffer, suffer into truth.
We cannot sleep, and drop by drop at the heart
the pain of pain remembered comes again,
and we resist, but ripeness comes as well.
From the gods enthroned on the awesome rowing-bench
there comes a violent love.[1]

Zeus has taught human beings to think about their predicament: we cannot forget our pain; even in sleep, the memory of past sorrow drips ceaselessly into our hearts. Men and women may try to resist the law of suffering, but the gods have ordained that their reflective powers will set them on the path to wisdom, ripeness, and blessing.

In *Eumenides,* the last play of the trilogy, Aeschylus shows us humanity's passage from the brutal violence of a tribal, kin-based society, with its inexorable, self-destructive ethic of revenge, to life in a civilized city (*polis*), where crime is judged by the rational process of law. Still in flight from the Furies, Orestes arrives in Athens and flings himself at the feet of its patronal deity Athena. She convenes the city council to decide his fate by the due process of law. The Furies argue that Orestes must pay for his crime, but the jury is split and Athena has the casting vote. She acquits Orestes but placates the Furies by offering them a shrine in the city, decreeing that henceforth they will be known as the Eumenides, "the Compassionate Ones." The polis can be seen as a symbol of the rational new brain that enables us to hold aloof from the instinctive drives of the old brain and take responsibility for them. In their long-term effects, the dark deeds of the past live on in the polis, so Athenians must acknowledge them and make a place for them in their minds and hearts; they can then transform these primitive passions into a force for compassion.[2]

But when the old brain is co-opted by the new, the result can be disastrous. Reason was an ambiguous tool, because, as we have seen throughout history, it can be used to find a logically sound rationale for actions that violate our humanity. In his tragedy *Medea,* Euripides (c. 484–406 BCE) told the story of the eponymous woman from Colchis who married Jason, hero of the Argonauts, and helped him find the Golden Fleece. When Jason callously casts her off, in revenge Medea kills not only Jason and his new wife, but the children she and Jason conceived together. Very few animals would slaughter their young, yet Medea is driven to this act by her uniquely human reasoning powers. Arguing with the consummate logic that Athenians were developing in their democratic assemblies, she raises one objection to her hideous plan after another, only to reach a terrifying conclusion: she cannot punish Jason as he deserves unless she also murders their boys. She is too intelligent not to find the most effective means of revenge and too tough not to carry it out.[3] If it is not tempered by compassion and empathy, reason can lead men and women into a moral void.

But it was also true, as Aristotle (384–322 BCE) would claim later, that the exercise of our rational powers was essential to the empathetic experience of tragic drama. Without the detached critical rigor that enabled you to stand back from the reptilian me-first mentality, you would be unable to escape from your self-preoccupation and appreciate the plight of another person. Tragedy, Aristotle believed, educated the emotions and taught people to experience them appropriately. As he watched the drama unfold, a small-minded person would see his own troubles in perspective and an arrogant person would learn to feel compassion for the unfortunate. Purified, drained of their dangerous potential, the emotions could thus become beneficial to the community.[4]

We are a tragic species, divided against ourselves, our two brains locked in conflict. As they learned to identify with the suffering hero, the Greek audience found themselves weeping for people they might otherwise shun—for Medea or for Heracles, who in a fit of divinely inspired madness killed his wife and children. At the end of Euripides' *Heracles,* Theseus, legendary king of Athens, embraces the broken man and leads him gently offstage, the two bound together "in a yoke of friendship." As they bid him farewell, the chorus laments Heracles' fate "with mourning and with many tears . . . For we today have lost our noblest friend."[5] The art of the dramatist enabled the audience to achieve an expansion of sympathy, so that they had a taste of the "immeasurable" power of compassion. An audience that could befriend a man who had committed an act like that of Heracles had achieved a Dionysian *ekstasis,* a "stepping out" of ingrained preconceptions in an empathy that, before seeing the play, they would probably have deemed impossible.

In 430, at one of the darkest moments of the senseless and destructive Peloponnesian War, Sophocles (c. 496–

405 BCE) presented his tragedy *Oedipus the Tyrant* to the people of Athens. When reason failed, it was still possible for human beings to learn from their pain. Renowned for his clear-sighted wisdom, Oedipus proved fatally, tragically ignorant. To his horror, he discovers that not only has he unwittingly slain his father, but also, unaware of her true identity, that he has married his mother. His tragedy, however, gives him an entirely new vulnerability and, consequently, an ability to enter into the suffering of others.[6] His speech, hitherto reasoned and controlled, is now interspersed with wordless exclamations: *"Ion . . . ion! Aiai . . . aiai!"* When he meets his weeping daughters, he forgets his own distress in concern for their plight. The members of the chorus make their own journey to compassion. Initially appalled by Oedipus's predicament, they cannot bear to look at him and shrink away in horror, but as they learn to appreciate the depth of his grief, this revulsion gives way to affection; they show the audience how to react to his tragedy as they reach out to Oedipus, calling him "dear one" and "darling."[7] In *Oedipus at Colonus,* which Sophocles presented at the end of his life, Oedipus, a man shunned for his unspeakable but unintentional crimes, becomes a source of blessing to the citizens of Athens when they have the compassion to take him in and give him asylum.[8]

Tragic drama reminds us of the role that art can play in expanding our sympathies. Plays, films, and novels all enable us to enter imaginatively into other lives and make an empathetic identification with people whose experiences are entirely different from our own. They can give us moments of compassionate *ekstasis,* and we should resolve, during this step, to allow art to unsettle us and make us question ingrained preconceptions. Films are especially emotive, because the big screen brings us even closer to the characters. We can find ourselves moved to tears, our mirror neurons firing as we witness the pain of characters in a movie, even though our rational minds tell us that their suffering is entirely fictional. When we have been affected in this way, we should not be too hasty to forget the experience as we leave the cinema or put the novel back on the shelf. We should let the pathos lodge permanently in our minds, in the same way as Athens made a home for both Oedipus and the Eumenides.

Imagination is crucial to the compassionate life. A uniquely human quality, it enables the artist to create entirely new worlds and give a strong semblance of reality to events that never happened and people who never existed. Compassion and the abandonment of ego are both essential to art: it is easy to spot a poem, a novel, or a film that is self-indulgent or brittle with cruel cleverness. When a film makes us weep, it is often because it has touched a buried memory or unacknowledged yearning of our own. Art calls us to recognize our pain and aspirations and to open our minds to others. Art helps us—as it helped the Greeks—to realize that we are not alone; everybody else is suffering too.

The Greek dramatists were trying to sensitize their audience to pain. Instead of maintaining ourselves in a state of deliberate heartlessness in order to keep suffering at bay, we should open our hearts to the grief of others as though it were our own. The Tibetans call this quality *shen dug ngal wa la mi sö pa*, which means "the inability to bear the sight of another's sorrow." It is this, the Dalai Lama explains, that "compels us not to shut our eyes even when we want to ignore others' distress."[9] From early childhood, the theologian, doctor, and missionary Albert Schweitzer (1875–1965) was saddened by the misery that he saw around him, especially the suffering of animals. "The sight of an old limping horse, tugged forward by one man while another kept beating it with a stick to get it to the knacker's yard at Colmar, haunted me for weeks," he recalled.[10] He did not push the experience to the back of his mind or seek to repress it; rather, he allowed it to become a habitual memory, and this empathetic attitude would inspire him to devote his life to the alleviation of such hardship. In 1905, he decided to study medicine, a discipline that he did not find congenial, in order to practice as a doctor in Africa. "While at the university and enjoying the happiness of being able to study and even to produce some results in science and art," he explained, "I could not help thinking continually of others who were denied that happiness by their material circumstances or their health."[11]

The suffering we have experienced in our own life can also help us to appreciate the depths of other people's unhappiness. That is why it was important to revisit your own past pain during the third step. The dynamic of the Golden Rule is beautifully expressed in an early sura of the Qur'an in which God (referring to himself in the third person) asks Muhammad to remember the sorrows of his childhood—he had been orphaned as small child, parceled out to relatives, and for years was a marginalized member of his family and tribe—and make sure that nobody else in his community would endure this deprivation.

> *What is after will be better*
> *than what came before*
> *To you your lord will be giving*
> *You will be content*
>
> *Did he not find you orphaned*
> *And give you shelter*
> *Find you lost*
> *and guide you*
> *Find you in hunger*
> *and provide for you*
>
> *As for the orphan—*
> *do not oppress him*
> *And one who asks for help—*
> *do not turn him away*
> *And the grace of your lord—proclaim!*[12]

In this step, we begin to make this dynamic part of our own lives.

The experience of pain and humiliation has inspired people to heroic compassion. When Gandhi, a young Indian lawyer who had hitherto led a privileged life, was violently thrown off a train in South Africa, he became aware of the plight of Indians in the country: he had been sitting in a first-class carriage, which was forbidden to "colored" men, and refused to move. Within a week, he summoned all the Indians of Pretoria to a meeting, which marked the beginning of a lifelong, nonviolent campaign against oppression. Patty Anglin, who chairs the Children's Health Alliance of Wisconsin, has devoted her life to caring for children abandoned by their parents, many of them with special needs. She has always claimed that the misery she experienced in a harsh boarding school, where she had learning difficulties, prepared her for her life's work: "I would need to understand the feelings of abandonment, loneliness, fear, and the sense of not belonging—the same feelings that children from abusive, dysfunctional, and broken homes feel."[13]

Our pain, therefore, can become an education in compassion. Some people deliberately steel their hearts against involvement with other people's suffering: the bank manager must turn a deaf ear to the pleas of the insolvent borrower and cannot allow his distress to keep him awake at night, the businessperson has no option but to sack an inefficient employee, and the doctor cannot afford to become emotionally distraught each time a patient dies. It is natural to try to avoid unnecessary grief. During this step, we should take note of our initial reluctance to engage. We don't want to listen to the sad story that a colleague is telling us. We feel that we have enough to deal with and push her troubles from our mind. We can be irritated by somebody's bad mood instead of asking ourselves why she is depressed. We hurry past the homeless man outside the supermarket, refusing to allow his plight to disturb our equanimity. But when this happens, it is time to draw upon everything you learned in the last step and recall your *own* past distress. Remember the things that help you when *you* are having a bad day—a kind word, a smile, a joke—and try to give that gift to a testy colleague. Remember what it is like to feel alone with sadness and take the trouble to listen to your friend's tale of woe: "And one who asks for help—do not turn him away."

In this step, you are going to add three more stages to the meditation on the "immeasurable minds of love." Again, imagine yourself at the center of a series of concentric circles. Then, after you have directed your friendship, compassion, joy, and even-mindedness toward yourself, turn your attention to three individuals known to you. It is important to be specific or the exercise will degenerate into meaningless generalities. Call to mind in turn a person for whom you have no strong feelings one way or the other; somebody you like, such as a friend or family member; and finally a person you dislike. Call them by name; picture each one of them sitting beside you so that they are vividly present to you.

As you direct the four Immeasurables to each one of them in turn, think of their good points, their contribution to your own life; their generosity, courage, and sense of humor. Look deeply into their hearts, insofar as you can, and see their pain: the sufferings you are aware of and all the private sorrows that you will never know about. You will then desire them to be free of their pain and resolve to help them in any way you can. Wish for each of your three people the joy that you desire for yourself, and finally admit that you all have faults—yourself, the person you feel neutral toward, the one you like, as well as the one you find objectionable. You are striving for *upeksha,* the equanimity that enables you to relate to people impartially.

The meditation obviously becomes more difficult when you try to direct these thoughts of friendship, compassion, joy, and even-mindedness to the person you dislike. Stay with this difficulty and become fully aware of it, because it shows how limited your compassion is. We may think that we are compassionate people, but so much of our goodwill is dependent upon subjective likes and dislikes. Notice the angry thoughts that arise in your mind when you think of this individual and see how unattractive they are. Other people like her, so it is probable that your dislike stems entirely from her attitude toward *you.* Does she threaten your interests, get in your way, or behave in a manner that makes you think less well of yourself? If so, your dislike is probably based on the ego delusion we considered during the last step. There is nothing immutable or objective about friendship or enmity: nobody is born a friend or an enemy; last year's friend can become next year's enemy. She has good and bad qualities, just as you do. Like everybody else in the world, she longs for happiness and wishes to be free of pain. She suffers in ways that you will never know. How, therefore, can you single her out for your dislike and refuse to direct your feelings of friendship, compassion, joy, and even-mindedness to her?

Be patient with yourself during this meditation; do not become irritated if you are distracted or discouraged if you seem to make no progress. Do not feel guilty if you are unable to overcome your feelings of aversion. Practiced over time, this meditation can make a compassionate groove in your mind. It should become part of your daily practice throughout the remaining steps. It should be a relaxed, ruminative process. It need not—indeed, should not—take hours of your time. But if practiced faithfully, it will help you develop two new tools: a capacity for inwardness and the ability to think of others in the same way as you think of yourself. Only practice makes perfect, just as it takes years for a dancer to turn a perfect pirouette.

As you conclude the meditation, make a resolution that today you will translate these good thoughts into a small, concrete practical act of friendship or compassion to one of your three people, if you have the chance. If you do not see them, reach out to somebody else who needs a helping hand or a friendly word.

Mindfulness

As we practice the Immeasurables, we are bound to become aware of the selfishness that impedes our compassionate outreach, balks at the thought of extending friendship to an enemy, and rebels against the idea that "I" am neither unique nor exempt from life's ills. The purpose of mindfulness, one of the practices that brought the Buddha to enlightenment, is to help us to detach ourselves from the ego by observing the way our minds work. You might find it helpful to learn more about the neurological makeup of the brain and the way that meditation can enhance your sense of peace and interior well-being, so a few relevant books are listed in the Suggestions for Further Reading. But this is not essential. Practice is more important than theory, and you will find that it is possible to work on your mental processes just as you work out in the gym to enhance your physical fitness.

Mindfulness is form of meditation that we perform as we go about our daily lives, and is designed to give us more control over our minds so that we can reverse ingrained tendencies and cultivate new ones. This is what the Buddha did when he deliberately directed unhelpful emotions (such as greed, lust, or envy) into more positive channels. Just as musicians have to learn how to manipulate their instruments and an equestrienne requires an intimate knowledge of the horse she is training, we have to learn to use our mental energies more kindly and productively. This is not a meditation that we should perform in solitude, apart from our ordinary routines. In mindfulness we mentally stand back and observe our behavior while we are engaged in the normal process of living in order to discover more about the way we interact with people, what makes us angry and unhappy, how to analyze our experiences, and how to pay attention to the present moment. Mindfulness is not meant to make us morbidly self-conscious, scrupulous, or guilty; we are not supposed to pounce aggressively on the negative feelings that course through our minds. Its purpose is simply to help us channel them more creatively.

With mindfulness, we use our new analytical brain to step back and become aware of the more instinctive, automatic mental processes of the old brain. So we live in the moment, observing the way we speak, walk, eat, and think. The Tibetan word for meditation is *gom:* "familiarization." Mindfulness should give us greater familiarity with the Four Fs that are the cause of so much pain. We will become aware of how suddenly these impulses arise in response to stimuli that make us irrationally angry, hostile, greedy, rampantly acquisitive, lustful, or frightened, and how quickly they overturn the more peaceful, positive emotions. But instead of being overly distressed by this, we should recall that it is what nature intended and that these strong instinctual passions are simply working through us. Over time and with practice, we can learn how to become more aloof and refuse to identify with them: "This is not mine; this is not what I really am; this is not my self." But it will not happen overnight; we have to be patient and understand that there is no quick fix.

Yet we should also take careful note of how unhappy these primitive emotions make us. When you are engrossed in thoughts of anger, hatred, envy, resentment, or disgust, notice the way your horizons shrink and your creativity diminishes. I find it impossible to write well when I am churning with resentment. In the grip of these hostile preoccupations, we become focused on ourselves, can think of little else, and lose all wider perspective. We tend to assume that other people are the cause of our pain; with mindfulness, over time, we learn how often the real cause of our suffering is the anger that resides within us. When we are enraged, we tend to exaggerate a person's defects—just as when we are seized by desire we accentuate somebody's attractions and ignore her faults, even though at some level we may know that this is a delusion.

Similarly, we will become aware that the acquisitive drive, which originally motivated our search for food, is never satisfied. As you progress, you will notice that once a desire is fulfilled, you almost immediately start to want something else. If the object of your desire turns out to be disappointing, you become frustrated and unsettled. You soon realize that nothing lasts long. An irritation, idea, or fantasy that seemed all-consuming a moment ago tends to pass quite quickly, and before long you are distracted by a startling noise or a sudden drop in temperature, which shatters your concentration. We humans rarely sit absolutely still but are constantly shifting our position, even when we sleep. We suddenly get it into our heads to wander into another room, make a cup of tea, or find somebody to talk to. One minute we are seething over a colleague's inefficiency; the next we are daydreaming about our summer vacation. Gradually, as you become conscious of your changeability, you will find that you are beginning to sit a little more lightly to your opinions and desires. Your current preoccupation is not really "you," because in a few moments you will almost certainly be obsessing about something else.

This calm, dispassionate appraisal of our behavior helps us to become aware that our judgments are often biased and dependent on a passing mood, and that our endless self-preoccupation brings us into conflict with people who seem to get in our way. You will notice how easily and carelessly you inflict pain on others, sighing impatiently over a minor inconvenience, grimacing when the clerk is slow at the checkout, or raising your eyebrows in derision at what you regard as a stupid remark. But you will also see how upsetting it is when somebody behaves like that to *you*—and, conversely, that an unexpectedly kind or helpful act can brighten the day and change your mood in an instant.

Once we know that the cause of so much human pain is within ourselves, we have the motivation to change. We will find that we are happier when we are peaceful than when we are angry or restless, and that, like the Buddha, we can make the effort to cultivate these positive emotions, noticing, for example, that when we perform an act of kindness we ourselves feel better. Mindfulness should not make us anxious. Instead of being afraid of what will happen tomorrow, or wishing it was this time last week, we can learn to live more fully in the present. Instead of allowing a past memory to cloud our present mood, we can learn to savor simple pleasures—a sunset, an apple, or a joke. Mindfulness should be something that becomes habitual, but it is not an end in itself. It should segue naturally into action and could, after a few days, be profitably combined with the next step.

Action

On arrival at the House of Studies as a recently professed nun, I discovered that my new superior was dying of cancer. I was twenty years old, bruised by the abrasive training of the novitiate and eager for this new phase to begin, but things were starting to fall apart for me. Even though she was so sick, I was fortunate in my superior during this difficult time. She had had a hard life. She had been a promising school principal but, at the age of thirty, had suddenly become deaf, had to give up teaching, and was sent to work in the laundry room, where she remained for decades, folding towels and darning sheets. That would have made many people bitter—myself included—but she had not allowed this to sour her; she was one of the kindest people I had ever met. There was nothing sentimental about her, however; indeed, she was often quite fierce with us. She was also rather eccentric, so it was impossible to put her on a saintly pedestal. One afternoon, I remember, she got it into her head that the garden was in a deplorable state and sent us all out, in our long black habits, veils, and clattering rosary beads, into the driving rain to weed the flower beds, banging on the window to spur us on. And even though she herself was in constant pain, she was horrified to hear about my increasingly frequent bouts of nausea and nosebleeds. "Why didn't you *tell* me?" she asked in genuine distress. Despite her increasing debility, she took time to give me special lessons in logic, and was genuinely delighted when I got good reports from the tutors who were preparing me for the entrance examinations to Oxford University.

But finally she was taken to the Mother House to die. We young nuns all went into her room and stood around her bed to say good-bye. As she bade us farewell, she spoke of her imminent death with her usual pragmatism. "They've appointed a new superior for you, but she won't arrive until August!" she exclaimed, managing to laugh despite her obvious weakness and pain. "I'll be dead by then!" As we trooped out, she called me back and I went to kneel beside her bed. "Sister," she said, "when you came, I was told that you might be a problem. But I want you to know that you have never been a trouble to me. *You are a good girl, Sister.* Remember I told you so." I have never forgotten it. She was not saying anything cheesy, such as "I see future greatness in you": what she must have seen was a confused, immature, and rather tiresome young woman. It would have been so easy for her to close her eyes with relief as we left the room, take her pain medication, and sink back onto her pillow, but she made a valiant effort to reassure me because she could see that I was struggling.

I tell this story to show that one small act of kindness can turn a life around. I am quite sure that she must have forgotten the incident after an hour or two, but it has stayed with me all my life. In the troubled years that followed, I often recalled her words at particularly bleak moments. Indeed, I think of them still when I feel anything *but* good. The British poet William Wordsworth (1770–1850) wrote of iconic moments like this, which become a resource for us over the years:

> *There are in our existence spots of time,*
> *That with distinct pre-eminence retain*
> *A renovating virtue, whence, depressed*
> *By false opinion and contentious thought,*
> *Or aught of heavier or more deadly weight,*
> *In trivial occupations, and the round*
> *Of ordinary intercourse, our minds*
> *Are nourished and invisibly repaired.*[1]

My point is that we can all create "spots of time" for others, and that many of these will be the "little, nameless, unremembered, acts of kindness and of love" that, Wordsworth claimed in another poem, form "that best portion of a good man's life."[2]

As you embark on this step, try to think of "spots of time" in your own life, moments when somebody went out of his or her way to help you. You should also consider the effects of the unkind remarks that have been a corrosive presence in your mind over the years. They were all probably "nameless, unremembered," and insignificant to the people who uttered them, but they have the power to fester and assume an importance that the speaker probably never intended. We need to become aware that our impulsive words and actions have consequences that we could never have foreseen. So if you want to be a force for good in the world, you should apply the insights you gain in the practice of mindfulness to your daily dealings with others, shielding them from your destructive tendencies and trying to lighten their lives with acts of friendship.

We are not doomed to an existence of selfishness, because we have the ability, with disciplined, repetitive action, to construct new habits of thought, feeling, and behavior. If every time we are tempted to say something vile about an annoying sibling, a colleague, an ex-husband, or a country with whom we are at war, we reflexively ask ourselves "How would I like this said about me and mine?" and refrain, we will achieve *ekstasis,* a momentary "stepping outside" the egotistically confined self. If, as Confucius advised, we did this "all day and every day," we would be in a state of continuous *ekstasis,* which is not an exotic trance but the permanent selflessness of a Buddha or a sage. Skeptics argue that the Golden Rule just doesn't work, but they do not seem to have tried to implement it in a wholehearted and consistent way. It is not a notional doctrine that you either agree with or make yourself believe. It is a method—and the only adequate test of any method is to put it into practice. Throughout the centuries, people have found that when they behaved in accordance with the Golden Rule, they experienced a deeper, fuller level of existence, and they have maintained that anybody can achieve this state if she puts her mind to it.

But it will be a slow, incremental, and imperceptible process. First, make a resolution to act once every day in accordance with the *positive* version of the Golden Rule: "Treat others as you would wish to be treated yourself." This need not be a grand, dramatic gesture; it can be a "little, nameless, unremembered" act that may seem insignificant to you. Perhaps you make a point of giving an elderly relative a call, help your wife with the chores, or take time to listen to a colleague who is anxious or depressed. Look for an opportunity to create a "spot of time" in somebody's life, and this awareness will increase as you become more proficient in mindfulness. Second, resolve each day to fulfill the *negative* version of the Golden Rule: "Do not do to others what you would not like them to do to you." Try to catch yourself before you make that brilliantly wounding remark, asking yourself how *you* would like to be on the receiving end of such sarcasm—and refrain. Each time you succeed will be an *ekstasis,* a transcendence of ego. Third, make an effort once a day to change your thought patterns: if you find yourself indulging in a bout of anger or self-pity, try to channel all that negative energy into a more kindly direction. If you are in a rut of resentment, make an effort to think of something for which you know you should be grateful, even if you do not feel it at the time. If you are hurt by an unpleasant remark, remember that your own anger often issues from pain and that the person who spoke to you so unkindly may also be suffering.

As you brush your teeth or put the cat out at the end of the day, check to see if you have performed your three actions. Sometimes you will find that you have not done so; sometimes you will remember that, on the contrary, you have behaved unkindly and inconsiderately. At this point, recall what you learned during the third step and have compassion on yourself, smile wryly at your omission, and resolve to do better tomorrow. When these three actions have become habitual and part of your daily routine, it is time to up your game and try for *two* acts of kindness every day and to prevent yourself on *two* occasions from inflicting unnecessary pain. Then go for *three*—and so on. It will not be easy. The goal is to behave in this way "all day and every day." By that time, of course, you will have become a sage. . . .

How Little We Know

Quite early in my career, I was struck by a footnote in a book referring to the "science of compassion" that should characterize the work of a religious historian. This was not science in the sense of physics or chemistry, but a method of acquiring "knowledge" (Latin: *scientia*) by entering in a scholarly, empathetic way into the historical period that is being researched. Some of the religious practices of the past may sound bizarre to modern ears, but the historian has to "empty" herself of her own post-Enlightenment presuppositions, leave her twentieth-century self behind, and enter wholeheartedly into the viewpoint of a world that is very different from her own. A religious historian must not "substitute his own or his readers' conventions for the original," the author explained; rather, he should "broaden his perspective so that it can make place for the

other." He must not cease interrogating his material until "he has driven his understanding to the point where he
has an immediate human grasp of what a given position
meant" and, with this empathetic understanding of the
context, "could feel himself doing the same."[1]

I was at once impressed by the phrase "make place for
the other." When I tried to put this directive into practice
in my studies, I found that it entirely changed my con-
ception of religion. Hitherto I had tended to project my
twentieth-century assumptions onto the spiritualities of
the past, and not surprisingly, many had seemed absurd.
But when I tried to "broaden" my perspective in this disciplined and empathetic way, they gradually began to make
sense.[2] As this attitude became habitual (I was practicing
it at my desk for several hours every day), I began to notice how seldom we "make place for the other" in social
interaction. All too often people impose their own experience and beliefs on acquaintances and events, making
hurtful, inaccurate, and dismissive snap judgments, not
only about individuals but about whole cultures. It often
becomes clear, when questioned more closely, that their
actual knowledge of the topic under discussion could com-
fortably be contained on a small postcard. Western society
is highly opinionated. Our airwaves are clogged with talk
shows, phone-ins, and debates in which people are encouraged to express their views on a wide variety of subjects.
This freedom of speech is precious, of course, but do we
always know what we are talking about?

The immense achievements of modern science can lead
us to believe that we are steadily pushing back the fron-

tiers of ignorance and will soon lay bare the last secrets of the universe. Science is by its very nature progressive: it continually breaks new ground, and once a theory is disproved and surpassed, it is of only antiquarian interest. But the knowledge we acquire through the humanities and the arts does not advance in this way. Here we keep on asking the same questions—What is happiness? What is truth? How do we live with our mortality?—and rarely arrive at a definitive answer, because there *are* no definitive answers to these perennial problems. Each generation has to start over and find solutions that speak directly to its unique circumstances. Philosophers today still discuss the issues that preoccupied Plato.

The pursuit of knowledge is exhilarating, and science, medicine, and technology have dramatically improved the lives of millions of people. But unknowing remains an essential part of the human condition. Religion is at its best when it helps us to ask questions and holds us in a state of wonder—and arguably at its worst when it tries to answer them authoritatively and dogmatically. We can never understand the transcendence we call God, Nirvana, Brahman, or Dao; precisely because it *is* transcendent, it lies beyond the reach of the senses, and is therefore incapable of definitive proof. Certainty about such matters, therefore, is misplaced, and strident dogmatism that dismisses the views of others inappropriate. If we say that we know exactly what "God" is, we could well be talking about an idol, a deity we have created in our own image.

This appreciation of the limits of our knowledge also lies at the heart of the Western rational tradition, one of whose founding luminaries was Socrates (c. 470–399 BCE). Socrates believed that wisdom was not about accumulating information and reaching hard-and-fast conclusions. To his dying day, he insisted that the only reason he could be considered wise was because he knew that he knew nothing at all. When he was attacked by a leading Athenian politician, he told himself:

> I am wiser than this man; it is likely that neither of us knows anything worthwhile, but he thinks he knows something when he does not, whereas when I do not know, neither do I think that I know; so I am likely to be wiser than he to this small extent, that I do not think about what I do not know.[3]

The people who came to see Socrates usually thought that they knew what they were talking about, but after half an hour of his relentless questioning they discovered that they knew nothing at all about such basic issues as justice or courage. They felt deeply perplexed, like bewildered children; the intellectual and moral foundations of their lives had been radically undermined, and they experienced a frightening, vertiginous doubt (*aporia*). For Socrates, that was the moment when a person became a philosopher, a "lover of wisdom," because he had become aware that he longed for greater insight, knew he did not have it, but would henceforth seek it as ardently as a lover pursues his beloved.

Thus dialogue led participants not to certainty but to a shocking realization of the profundity of human ignorance. However carefully, logically, and rationally Socrates and his friends analyzed a topic, something always eluded them. Yet many found that the initial shock of *aporia* led to *ekstasis,* because they had "stepped outside" their former selves. Plato (c. 428–347 BCE), Socrates' most famous disciple, used the language associated with Mysteries of Eleusis to describe the moment when, pushed to the very limit of what was knowable, the mind tipped over into transcendence:

> It is only when all these things, names and definitions, visual and other sensations are rubbed together and subjected to tests in which questions and answers are exchanged in good faith and without malice that finally, when human capacity is stretched to its limit, a spark of understanding and intelligence flashes out and illuminates the subject at issue.[4]

As for the sages of India, this insight was the result of a dedicated way of life. It was, Plato went on to explain, "not something that can be put into words like other branches of learning; only after long partnership in a common life devoted to this very thing does truth flash upon the soul, like a flame kindled by a leaping spark, and once it is born there it nourishes itself hereafter."[5]

Socrates used to describe himself as a gadfly, stinging people to question every one of their ideas, especially those about which they felt certainty, so that they could wake up to a more accurate perception of themselves.[6] Even though he was conversing with Socrates and others, each participant was also engaged in a dialogue with himself, subjecting his own deeply held opinions to rigorous scrutiny before, finally, as a result of the ruthless logic of Socrates' questioning, relinquishing them. You entered into a Socratic dialogue in order to change; the object of the exercise was to create a new, more authentic self. After they had realized that some of their deepest convictions were based on faulty foundations, Socrates' disciples could begin to live in a philosophical manner. But if they did not interrogate their most fundamental beliefs, they would live superficial, expedient lives, because "the unexamined life is not worth living."[7]

The Chinese philosopher and mystic Zhuangzi (c. 370–311 BCE), one of the chief sages of the Axial Age, agreed that the only thing worth saying was a question that plunged listeners into doubt and numinous uncertainty. As a Daoist, Zhuangzi sought to bring his life into harmony with the Way (*dao*), by which he meant all the myriad patterns, forms, and potential that made nature the way it was. Yet while nature is in constant flux, we always go against the grain and try to freeze our ideas and experiences and make them absolute. It is egotism that makes us identify with one opinion rather than another, become quarrelsome and unkind, say *this* could not mean *that,* and think we have a duty to change others to suit ourselves.

Zhuangzi regarded the Confucians, who were constantly trying to persuade the rulers of China to adopt more compassionate policies, as interfering busybodies. Yet sometimes he mischievously put his own ideas into the mouth of Confucius and his disciples in stories he made up for the occasion. In one of these, Confucius's most advanced pupil,

Yan Hui, came to see his teacher and announced: "I'm gaining ground!" "What do you mean?" Confucius asked. Yan Hui explained proudly that he had completely forgotten all his master's teachings about *ren* and morality. "That's not it," said Confucius. A few days later, Yan Hui was delighted to tell the master that he had now forgotten all about the *li*. "Not bad," Confucius admitted, "but that's still not it." Finally, Yan Hui surprised him: "I'm gaining ground!" he said, beaming. "I sit quietly and forget." Confucius shifted uneasily. "What do you mean?" he asked. "I let the body fall away and let the intellect fade," replied Yan Hui. "I throw out form, abandon understanding—and then move freely, blending away into the great transformation. That's what I mean by *sit quietly and forget*." Realizing that his pupil had surpassed him, Confucius went pale. "If you blend away like that, you're free of likes and dislikes," he said. "So in the end, the true sage here is you! So you won't mind if I follow you from now on, will you?"[8]

When we cling to our certainties, likes, and dislikes, deeming them essential to our sense of self, we alienate ourselves from the "great transformation" of the Way, because the reality is that we are all in continual flux, moving from one state to another. An unenlightened person, Zhuangzi explained, is like a frog in a well who mistakes the tiny patch of sky he can see for the whole; but once he has seen the sky's immensity, his perspective is changed forever.[9] If we are determined to remain trapped in our current perspective, our understanding remains "small . . . cramped and busy." But the sage, who has left the ego behind, has achieved what Zhuangzi called the "Great Knowledge," which is "broad and unhurried."[10] You arrive at this only when you learn to "sit quietly and forget" one thing after another until finally you forget about yourself. Your heart will then be "empty" of bustling self-importance and, without the distorting lens of selfishness, it will reflect other things and people like a mirror.[11] This "emptiness" leads naturally to empathy. "The perfect man has no self," Zhuangzi explained.[12] Once he has lost the belief that he is special and particular, he regards all other people as "I." "People cry, so he cries—he considers everything as his own being."[13] Zhuangzi was a hermit, and his views were sometimes deliberately expressed in an extreme form to shock his listeners into fresh insights, but he resembled Socrates in his insistence that we should hold aloof from the opinionated ego. His art of forgetting is close to the "science of compassion" I described earlier, with its discipline of emptying the mind of culturally conditioned preconceptions in order to "make place for the other." If our view of others is perpetually clouded by our own prejudices, opinions, needs, and desires, we will neither understand nor truly respect them.

Today unknowing no longer seems obscurantist. As we have seen, so many of the things we once took for granted have proved unreliable that we may have to "forget" old ways of thought in order to meet the current challenges. At the beginning of the twentieth century, physicists believed that there were only a few unresolved problems in the Newtonian system before our knowledge of the universe would be complete. But a mere twenty years later, quantum mechanics exploded old certainties and unveiled a universe that was indeterminate and unknowable. As the American physicist Percy Bridgman (1882–1961) explained:

> The structure of nature may eventually be such that our processes of thought do not correspond to it sufficiently to permit us to think about it at all. . . . The world fades out and eludes us. . . . We are confronted with something truly ineffable. We have reached the limit of the great pioneers of science, the vision, namely, that we live in a sympathetic world in that it is comprehensible to our minds.[14]

Yet physicists have not felt frustrated by contemplating the unknowable. The cosmologist Paul Davies has described the joy he experiences when delving into unanswerable questions. "Why did we come to exist 13.7 billion years ago in a Big Bang? Why are the laws of electromagnetism or gravitation as they are? Why these laws? What are we doing here? . . . It's truly astonishing."[15] The philosopher Karl Popper (1902–94) often remarked "We don't know anything" and believed that this was the most important philosophical truth.[16] But far from being depressed by his lack of knowledge, he actually reveled in it: "One of the many great sources of happiness is to get a glimpse, here and there, of a new aspect of the incredible world we live in and of our incredible role in it."[17] Albert Einstein (1879–1955) experienced mystical wonder when he contemplated the universe:

To know that what is impenetrable to us really exists, manifesting itself to us as the highest wisdom and the most radiant beauty, which our dull faculties can comprehend only in their most primitive forms—this knowledge, this feeling is at the center of all true religiousness. In this sense, and in this sense only, I belong to the ranks of devoutly religious men.[18]

He was convinced that "he to whom this emotion is a stranger . . . is as good as dead."[19] Albert Schweitzer might have agreed. When he looked back on his life, he saw that one of its guiding perceptions had been the "realization that the world is inexplicably mysterious."[20]

At their most insightful, the religions have insisted that the core of each man and woman eludes our grasp and is transcendent. This is where we discover Nirvana, Brahman, and what the German-born Protestant theologian Paul Tillich (1886–1965) called the very Ground of Being; we find the Kingdom of Heaven within us and discover that Allah is closer to us than our jugular vein. The Renaissance humanists developed a profound respect for the wonder of the human being, and their vision is beautifully expressed by William Shakespeare (1564–1616), when he makes his tragic hero Hamlet cry:

What a piece of work is a man! How noble in reason! How infinite in faculties! in form and moving, how express and admirable! in action, how like an angel! in apprehension, how like a god! the beauty of the world! the paragon of animals![21]

Even though each human being is a "quintessence of dust," a moribund and in many ways tragic creature,[22] he or she remains a godlike marvel and should be accorded absolute respect.

Hindus acknowledge this when they greet each other by bowing with joined hands to honor the sacred mystery they are encountering. Yet most of us fail to express this reverence for others in our daily lives. All too often we claim omniscience about other people, other nations, other cultures, and even those we claim to love, and our views about them are frequently colored by our own needs, fears, ambitions, and desires. This is beautifully expressed in another passage from *Hamlet*. The prince is causing a great deal of trouble in the Danish court, and the king has employed two of his old friends, Rosencrantz and Guildenstern, to spy on him. It does not take Hamlet long to realize what is going on, and one evening he presents Guildenstern with a pipe and tells him to play it. "My lord, I cannot!" Guildenstern replies. "It is as easy as lying," Hamlet remarks caustically, and goes on to insist that it is a simple matter of blowing through the mouthpiece and putting your fingers over the stops. "I have not the skill," Guildenstern protests. "Why, look you now," says Hamlet bitterly,

> how unworthy a thing you make of me! You would play upon me; you would seem to know my stops; you would pluck out the heart of my mystery; you would sound me from my lowest note to the top of my compass. . . . Do you think I am easier to be played on than this pipe?[23]

Instead of discoursing confidently on other people's motives, intentions, and desires, we should recall the essential "mystery" and realize that there is a certain sacrilege in attempting to "pluck out" its heart to serve an agenda of our own.

Quoting the French philosopher Simone Weil (1903–43), Iris Murdoch (1919–99) used to say that love was the sudden realization that somebody else absolutely exists. It is a theme that runs through many of her novels. She often describes a character shocked into a perception of the "mystery" of another object or person, which is unexpectedly revealed as marvelously separate from himself or herself. Here a self-absorbed, somewhat superficial girl, a former art student, visits the National Gallery in London during a personal crisis and discovers that she is moved by the pictures in a new way:

> Here was something that her consciousness could not wretchedly devour, and by making it part of her fantasy make it worthless. Even [her estranged husband], she thought, only existed now as someone she dreamt about; or else as a vague external menace never really encountered and understood. But the pictures were something real outside herself, which spoke to her kindly and yet in sovereign tones, something superior and good whose presence destroyed the dreary, trance-like solipsism of her earlier mood. When the world had seemed to be subjective it had seemed to be without interest or value. But now there was something in it after all.[24]

Such an experience is an *ekstasis* that releases us from the prison of selfhood.

The aim of this step is threefold: (1) to recognize and appreciate the unknown and unknowable, (2) to become sensitive to overconfident assertions of certainty in ourselves and other people, and (3) to make ourselves aware of the numinous mystery of each human being we encounter during the day.

First, think about those experiences that touch you deeply and lift you momentarily beyond yourself so that you seem to inhabit your humanity more fully than usual. It may be listening to a particular piece of music, reading certain poems, looking at a beautiful view, or sitting quietly with someone you love. Spend a little time each day enjoying this *ekstasis* and notice how difficult it is to speak of your experience or to say exactly what it is that moves you. Try to explain to somebody precisely how it has this effect on you, what it is telling you, and listen to the inadequacy of your words. Investigate the theme of unknowing in human experience. If you are scientifically inclined, you can explore the indeterminate universe of quantum mechanics, the neurological complexity of the mind, or depth psychology.

Second, stand back and listen to the aggressive certainty that characterizes so much of our discourse these days. Consider your profession or something that really interests you: literature, the law, economics, sports, pop music, medicine, or history. Isn't it true that the more you know about this special field of yours, the more acutely you become aware of all you still have to learn? Then notice how disturbing it is to hear somebody talking dogmatically about your subject over dinner or on the radio, making serious mistakes and false claims that are almost physically painful to hear.

When you listen to talk shows and phone-ins or to politicians arguing with one another, do you think these people really know what they are talking about? Are they able to see both sides of an argument? Are they identifying themselves too closely with their own opinions, in the way Zhuangzi suggested, so that self-interest is clouding their judgment? Are they more interested in scoring points than seeking the truth? Does anybody ever say "I don't know"? What would Socrates have made of these discussions?

As an exercise in open-mindedness, select one of your most deeply held opinions—about politics, religion, the economy, football, movies, music, or business—and make a list of everything you know that supports your viewpoint. Then make a list of arguments that contradict it. If you are in a reading discussion group, conduct a debate in which everybody argues for a position that is the opposite of what he or she believes. Then discuss your experience. What does it feel like to enter into another perspective? Did you learn something that you didn't know before? What do you think Socrates meant when he said, "The unexamined life is not worth living"?

Third, spend some time trying to define exactly what distinguishes you from everybody else. Delve beneath your everyday consciousness: Do you find your true self—what the Upanishads called the *atman*? Or does this self constantly elude you? Then ask yourself how you think you can possibly talk so knowingly about the self of other people. As part of your practice of mindfulness, notice how often you contradict yourself and act or speak in a manner that surprises you so that you say, "Now why did I do that?" Try to describe the essence of your personality to somebody else. Write down a list of your qualities, good and bad. And then ask yourself whether it really sums you up.

Make a serious attempt to pin down precisely what it is that you love about your partner or a close friend. List that person's qualities: Is that why you love him? Or is there something about her that you cannot describe? During your mindfulness practice, look around your immediate circle: your family, colleagues, and friends. What do you *really* know about each and every one of them? What are their deepest fears and hopes? What are their most intimate dreams and fantasies? And how well do you think they really know you?

Meditate on Hamlet's words to Guildenstern. How many people could say to *you* that you "pluck out the heart of my mystery"? In your mindfulness practice, notice how often, without thinking, you try to manipulate, control, or exploit others—sometimes in tiny and apparently unimportant ways. How often do you belittle other people in your mind to make them fit *your* worldview? Notice how upsetting it is when you become aware that somebody is trying to manipulate or control you, or when somebody officiously explains your thoughts and actions to you, plucking out the heart of *your* mystery.

How Should We Speak to One Another?

Dialogue is one of the buzzwords of our time. There is widespread conviction that if only people would enter into dialogue, peace would break out. But there is very little Socratic dialogue in the world today. Our discourse tends to be aggressive, a tradition we inherited from the ancient Greeks. In the democratic assemblies of Athens, citizens learned to debate competitively, to marshal arguments logically and effectively, and to argue their case against one another in order to *win*. They practiced rhetorical ploys to undermine their opponents' position and had no qualms about discrediting them and their cause in order to marginalize their policies. The object was to defeat one's opponent: nobody was expected to change his mind, be converted to the other side, or enter empathetically into the rival viewpoint.

As we have seen, the type of dialogue invented by Socrates was quite different. Like all Athenians, Socrates had taken part in these debates, and he did not like them.[1] If he were one of those "clever and disputatious debaters," he told the ambitious young aristocrat Meno, he would simply state his opinion and ask Meno to refute it. But this was not appropriate in a dialogue between people who "are friends, as you and I are, and want to discuss with each other." In true dialogue, participants "must answer in a manner more gentle and more proper to discussion."[2] The Socratic dialogue was a spiritual exercise designed to produce a profound psychological change in the participants, and because its purpose was that each person should understand the depth of his ignorance, there was no way that anybody could win.

Plato described the dialogue as a communal meditation that was hard work, requiring "a great expense of time and trouble," but like his master, he insisted that it be conducted in a kindly, compassionate manner. It would not bring transcendent insight unless "questions and answers are exchanged in good faith and without malice."[3] Nobody must be pushed into a position about which he felt uncomfortable. Each participant should make a "place for the other" in his mind, listening intently and sympathetically to the ideas of his partners in dialogue and allowing them to unsettle his own convictions. In return, they would permit their minds to be informed and changed by his contribution.

Both the Buddha and Confucius seem to have conducted discussion in a similar manner. Confucius always developed his insights in conversation with other people, because in his view we needed this friendly interaction to achieve maturity. In Chinese script, *ren* had two elements: the simple ideogram of a human being and two horizontal strokes indicating human relations. *Ren* can, therefore, be translated as "cohumanity."[4] But this cooperation required *ren*'s "softness" and "pliability," and Confucius would probably have appreciated the ritual of the Socratic dialogue, which demanded that participants "yield" to one another instead of holding rigidly to their own opinions. In the Analects, we see him mildly scolding his pupils, pushing them to the limit of their ability but never bullying them. Easygoing, affable, and calm, Confucius listened to them carefully and was always ready to concede their point of view. He was no sage, he would protest; his only talent was an "unwearying effort to learn and unflagging patience in teaching others."[5]

The Buddha too taught his monks to converse kindly and courteously with one another. His lay disciple King Pasenadi of Kosala was extremely impressed by the friendliness of the Buddhist community, which was in marked contrast to the royal court, where everybody was on the lookout for himself and chronically quarrelsome. When he sat with his council, he complained, he was constantly interrupted and sometimes even heckled. But when he visited the Buddha, he saw monks "living together as uncontentiously as milk with water and looking at one another with kind eyes . . . smiling, courteous, sincerely happy . . . their minds remaining as gentle as wild deer."[6] One day he told the Buddha about a conversation with his wife in which they had both admitted that nothing was more important to them than their own selves. Instead of lecturing the king on the "unskilful" nature of egotism or launching into a discussion of *anatta*, he entered into Pasenadi's position, starting from where his disciple actually was rather than where the Buddha thought he ought to be. He suggested that if the king found that there was nothing dearer to him than himself, he should reflect that everybody else felt exactly the same. Therefore, the Buddha concluded, giving Pasenadi his version of the Golden Rule, "A person who loves the self should not harm the self of others."[7]

Like Socrates, the Buddha believed that knowledge was a process of self-discovery. You did not gain insight by accepting the opinions of other people but by finding the truth within yourself. Even laypeople could achieve this. The Kalamans, a tribal people living on the northernmost fringe of the Ganges basin who were trying to find their place in the new urban civilization, sent a delegation to the Buddha. They were utterly confused: one teacher after another had descended upon them, but each simply promoted his own teachings and poured scorn on all the others. How could they tell who was right? "Come, Kalamans," the Buddha said, "do not be satisfied with hearsay or taking truth on trust." Instead of reeling off his own dharma and giving the poor bewildered Kalamans yet another doctrine to puzzle over, he told them that they were expecting other people to give them the answer when, if they looked into their own minds, they would find that they knew it already. Step by step, he helped them to draw upon their own experience: Was greed good or bad? Had they not noticed that when somebody was consumed by greed, he could become aggressive and even steal or lie? And had they observed that hatred simply made the hater unhappy? Yes, the Kalamans had noticed all this. So, the Buddha concluded, they had not needed him at all: they knew his dharma already. If instead of giving rein to their hatred and greed they tried to live more kindly and generously, they would find that they were happier.[8]

We do not engage in many dialogues like this today. The debates in our parliamentary institutions, the media, academia, and the law courts are essentially competitive. It is not enough for us to seek the truth; we also want to defeat and even humiliate our opponents. The malice and bullying tactics decried by Socrates are embraced with enthusiasm as part of the fun. A great deal of this type of discourse is a display of ego. There is no question of anybody admitting that she does not know the answer or has doubts about the validity of her case—even about complex issues for which there are no easy answers. Admitting that your opponents may have a valid point seems unthinkable. The last thing anybody intends is a change of mind. But while aggressive debate may be useful in politics, it is unlikely to transform hearts and minds—especially when an issue arouses passions that are already bitter and entrenched.

In our highly contentious world, we need to develop a twenty-first-century form of Socrates' compassionate discourse. For some years now, I have tried to counter the stereotypical view of Islam that has been current in the West for centuries but has become more prevalent since the atrocities of September 11, 2001. Like any received idea, it is based on what the Buddha called "hearsay" rather than accurate knowledge or understanding. So when politicians or pundits have insisted that Islam is an inherently violent, intolerant faith or inveigh furiously against the practice of veiling, for example, I have written articles, based on my study of Islamic history, to challenge this. But I have recently decided that this is counterproductive. All that happens is that my article is virulently attacked and my assailants rehearse the old ideas again with greater venom. As a result, the intellectual atmosphere becomes even more polluted and people remain entrenched in angry negativity. As the Daoists pointed out, we often identify with our ideas so strongly that we feel personally assaulted if these are criticized or corrected. Perhaps it would be better to take a leaf out of the Buddha's book and start from where people actually are rather than where we think they ought to be. In such public debates, instead of trying to bludgeon other people into accepting our own point of view, we may need to find a way of posing Socratic questions that lead to personal insight rather than simply repeating the facts as we see them yet again.

We should make a point of asking ourselves whether we want to win the argument or seek the truth, whether we are ready to change our views if the evidence is sufficiently compelling, and whether we are making "place for the other" in our minds in the Socratic manner. Above all, we need to listen. All too often in an argument or debate, we simply listen to others in order to twist their words and use them as grist for our own mill. True listening means more than simply hearing the words that are spoken. We have to become alert to the underlying message too and hear what is *not* uttered aloud. Angry speech in particular requires careful decoding. We should make an effort to hear the pain or fear that surfaces in body language, tone of voice, and choice of imagery.

To take just one example: every fundamentalist movement that I have studied in Judaism, Christianity, and Islam is rooted in a profound fear of annihilation; and each one began with what was perceived to be an assault by the liberal or secular establishment.[9] History shows that to attack any fundamentalist movement, whether militarily, politically, or in the media, is counterproductive because the assault merely convinces its adherents that their enemies really are bent on their destruction. If we analyze fundamentalist discourse as carefully as we interpret a poem or an important political speech, ferreting out the underlying emotions and intentions of the poet or speaker, this fear and humiliation become immediately apparent. Instead of ridiculing fundamentalist mythology, we should reflect seriously on the fact that it often expresses anxieties that no society can safely ignore. It is difficult to achieve this kind of dispassion, because any fundamentalist position is a profound challenge to principles and ideals, such as free speech or the rights of women, that are sacred to their liberal opponents. But aggression, righteous condemnation, and insult only make matters worse. Somehow we have to break the escalating cycle of attack and counterattack. We have seen what happens when fundamentalist fear hardens into rage.

Language is based on trust. We have to assume, at least

initially, that our interlocutor is speaking the truth and telling us something of value. Logicians have argued that the truth of an individual sentence can be assessed only by considering the whole context. It cannot be seen in isolation but is part of a "conceptual scheme," a fabric of interwoven sentences. We cannot understand the ideas expressed unless we are familiar with this conceptual scheme in its entirety.[10] Thus the sentence "the law is an ass" is explicable only in a particular framework. Linguists point out that in day-to-day communication, when we hear a statement that at first seems odd or false, we automatically try to find a context in which it makes sense, because we *want* to understand what is being said to us. The same mechanism is at work when we try to translate a text written in a foreign language. Linguists have called this epistemological law the "principle of charity"; it requires that when we are confronted with discourse that is strange to us, we seek an "interpretation which, in the light of what it knows of the facts, will maximise truth among the sentences of the corpus."[11]

In other words, when making an effort to understand something strange and alien to you, it is important to assume that the speaker shares the same human nature as yourself and that, even though your *belief systems* may differ, you both have the same idea of what constitutes *truth*. As Donald Davidson (1917–2003), professor of philosophy at the University of California, Berkeley, explains, "Making sense of the utterances and behaviour of others, even their most aberrant behaviour, requires us to find a great deal of truth and reason in them."[12] If we cannot do that, we will dismiss the speaker as irrational, nonsensical, and basically inhuman. "Charity," Davidson continues, "is forced on us, whether we like it or not; if we want to understand others, we must count them right in most matters."[13] This is how Jews such as Philo of Alexandria (c. 30 BCE to c. 45 CE), who were trained in Greek philosophy, approached the Torah. Instead of dismissing these ancient Hebrew texts as barbaric, they devised an allegorical interpretation that made them right according to their own Hellenistic standards, translating them into a more familiar idiom. They could not have achieved this had they not made a charitable assumption when studying these scriptures and finding thus a good deal of truth and reason in them.[14]

The "principle of charity" and the "science of compassion" are both crucial to any attempt to understand discourse and ideas that initially seem baffling, distressing, and alien; we have to re-create the entire context in which such words are spoken—historical, cultural, political, intellectual—question them deeply, and, as the footnote on the "science of compassion" advised, drive our understanding to the point where we have "an immediate human grasp of what a given position meant." With this new empathetic understanding of the context, we will find that we can imagine ourselves, in similar circumstances, feeling the same. In other words, we have to see where people are coming from. In this way, we can broaden our perspective and "make place for the other." We can ignore this compassionate imperative only if we do *not* wish to understand other people—an ethically problematic position.

There are of course times when we are required to be assertive. Even when we have gone through this process and understood the context in which a terrorist conceived his idea, we cannot, if we take the Golden Rule as our criterion, condone the course of action he has chosen. We have, however, broadened our horizons by developing an informed understanding of the possible frustration, humiliation, and despair of his situation and can now empathize with the plight of many of his innocent compatriots and coreligionists, who may feel something similar but have not resorted to criminal vengeance. Yet we must still dissociate ourselves from his atrocity. Nor should the "principle of charity" make us passive and supine in the face of injustice, cruelty, and discrimination. As we develop our compassionate mind, we should feel an increasing sense of responsibility for the suffering of others and form a resolve to do everything we can to free them from their pain. But it is no good responding to injustice with hatred and contempt. This, again, will simply inspire further antagonism and make matters worse. When we speak out in the defense of decent values, we must make sure that we understand the context fully and do not dismiss the values of our opponents as barbaric simply because they seem alien to us. We may find that we have the same values but express them in a radically different way.

How do we assert a strongly felt conviction with compassion? Saint Paul provides us with a useful checklist in the famous description of love quoted earlier. Charity is "patient and kind"; it "is never boastful, never conceited, never rude," never envious or "quick to take offence." Charity "keeps no score of wrongs" and "takes no pleasure in

the wrongdoing of others."[15] If we *are* quick to take of-
fense and positively smack our lips in self-righteous delight at the wrongdoing of others, we will fail this test. If
we speak impatiently, rudely, or unkindly, we may be in
danger of bringing ourselves down to the level of intolerance we are condemning. An older translation rendered
the phrase "never boastful, never conceited" as "charity . . .
is not puffed up." Our critique should not inflate the ego.
Sometimes when people are inveighing against an abuse or
crime, they seem almost to swell before our eyes with deli-
cious self-congratulation.

Gandhi left us a fine example of compassionate asser-
tiveness: advocating nonviolent resistance, he frequently
asked people to consider whether they fought to change
things or to punish. When Jesus told his followers to turn
the other cheek, Gandhi believed, he was urging them to
show courage in the face of hostility. This was the way to
transform hatred and contempt into respect. But nonviolence did not mean compliance with injustice: his opponents could have his dead body, Gandhi would insist, but
not his obedience.

During this step, we try to make ourselves mindful of
the way we speak to others. When you argue, do you get
carried away by your own cleverness and deliberately inflict pain on your opponent? Do you get personal? Will the
points you make further the cause of understanding or are
they exacerbating an already inflammatory situation? Are
you really listening to your opponent? What would happen if—while debating a trivial matter that would have no
serious consequences—you allowed yourself to lose the

argument? After a contentious discussion, conduct a post-mortem with yourself: Can you really back up everything you said in the heat of the moment? Did you *want* to inflict pain? Did you really know what you were talking about, or were you depending on hearsay? And before you embark on an argument or a debate, ask yourself honestly if you are ready to change your mind.

THE NINTH STEP

Concern for Everybody

So far we have confined our attention to the immediate community. But as we saw at the very beginning, this is not enough. Some religious traditions are more pluralistic than others, but all have at least one strand that insists that we cannot confine our compassion to our own group: we must also reach out in some way to the stranger and the foreigner—even to the enemy. Mozi put it clearly when he insisted that the well-being of humanity was dependent upon *jian ai:* "concern for everybody," a principled and practically oriented acknowledgment of the absolute equality of human beings. It is now time to apply what we have learned to the wider global community.

At an early stage of its development, tribalism enabled the human race to survive in harsh and inhospitable circumstances, but tribal chauvinism can be extremely dangerous.

The Prophet Muhammad's greatest political achievement was to find a way of helping the Arabs to transcend the aggressive *jahiliyyah* that was tearing Arabia apart. In the Qur'an, God tells humanity, "Behold, we have created you all out of a male and a female and have formed you into tribes and nations so that you may get to know one another."[1] Pluralism and diversity are God's will; the evolution of human beings into national and tribal groups was meant to encourage them to appreciate and understand the essential unity and equality of the entire human family. But national or tribal chauvinism (*asibiyyah*), which regards one's own group as inherently superior to all others, is condemned as arrogant and divisive. Tribalism in this sense is still alive and well today. If we continue to make our national interest an absolute value, to see our cultural heritage and way of life as supreme, and to regard outsiders and foreigners with suspicion and neglect their interests, the interconnected global society we have created will not be viable. After the world wars, genocide, and terrorism of the twentieth century, the purpose of the tribe or the nation can no longer be to fight, dominate, exploit, conquer, colonize, occupy, kill, convert, or terrorize rival groups. We have a duty to get to know one another, and to cultivate a concern and responsibility for *all* our neighbors in the global village.

During this step, we begin to expand our horizons to make place for the more distant other. Understanding different national, cultural, and religious traditions is no longer a luxury; it is now a necessity and must become a priority. The Dalai Lama has pointed out that when countries, continents, and even villages were economically and socially independent and contacts between them few, the destruction of an enemy could have been advantageous for "us":

> But we are now so interdependent that the concept of war has become outdated. . . . One-sided victory is no longer relevant. We must strive for reconciliation and always remember the interests of others. We cannot destroy our neighbours or ignore their interests! This would ultimately lead to our own suffering.[2]

In the global economy and the electronic age, national boundaries are becoming increasingly irrelevant; we can no longer simply draw a line in the sand between "us" and "them." War has an adverse effect on the financial markets; hundreds of thousands of civilians are likely to be killed; and the spectacle of their suffering is likely to inspire further terrorist atrocities, so if we harm our neighbors, we also inflict damage on ourselves.

There is often a reluctance to engage seriously with the problems of other nations. In fact, there has been an upsurge of nationalism and patriotic chauvinism. In the United Kingdom, we now have Scottish, Welsh, and Northern Irish parliaments. In Europe, there are rising fears that the influx of foreign workers who are deemed essential to the economy will dilute the national ethos. In the United States, the federal government has built a wall to keep illegal Mexican immigrants from entering the country. In the world of religion too, many people enjoy contact

with other faiths, but others have retreated into denomi-
national ghettos and erected new barriers of orthodoxy
against the "other." The strain of piety popularly known as
"fundamentalism" can be seen as a religiously articulated
form of nationalism or ethnicity, which emphasizes the
more particularistic elements of faith.

The stranger fills many of us with alarm. Yet unless the
oil gives out, the process of globalization seems irrevers-
ible, and this means that whether we like it or not, our
societies will become more multicultural. Like any major
political or social transformation, this will be painful. The
inhabitants of countries that were colonized by the Europeans in the nineteenth and twentieth centuries knew
how profoundly distressing it was to watch a cherished
way of life disappearing and beloved traditions decried by
powerful, disdainful foreigners. Now that we are living
side by side with people who may be at a different stage
of the modernization process, there will inevitably be tensions as we seek to accommodate one another. The Salman
Rushdie affair, for example, was a clash between two different conceptions of what is sacred: for the liberals, free
speech (the product in part of the modern economy) was
inviolable; for some members of the Muslim community,
however, for whom absolute freedom of speech was an unfamiliar concept, the priority was still the sovereignty of
God. It was a clash of orthodoxies in which neither side
could understand the viewpoint of the other.[3]

Somehow we have to find a more mature and compassionate way of negotiating these conflicts. Each side
needs to recognize that it threatens its opponents at a

profound and almost visceral level. In the biblical book of Leviticus, the priestly authors quote an early law code: "If a stranger lives with you in your land do not molest him. You must count him as one of your own countrymen and love him as yourself—for you were once strangers yourselves in Egypt."[4] Israelites must recall their own suffering as despised aliens in Egypt and ensure that the strangers currently in their midst do not endure this pain. Many immigrants to the West come from former European colonies and protectorates; those who resent their presence should consider that their distress is minimal compared with the massive disruption that occurred when the colonialists arrived and changed these countries forever. By the same token, immigrants should remember this pain and try to develop an empathy with those who fear that their own values will be eroded.

With the global situation in mind, consider the arguments Mozi developed against warfare, showing that it was of no benefit to anybody. How could these be adapted to the twenty-first century? We need to ask ourselves some hard questions to which there are no easy answers. You may want to debate them—compassionately and Socratically, of course!—in your reading discussion group. Think carefully about the concept of a just war. Find some examples of a just war in the past and then ask yourself how many of our current conflicts fit the just-war criteria. Can you detect the tribal spirit in any of them? Is military action improving the situation or is it increasing hostility? Given the shattering power of modern weaponry, do you think that warfare can ever be just or beneficial today? Can you apply some of Gandhi's ideas to a modern conflict? How would a nonviolent campaign work, and what qualities of mind and heart would it require?

During this step, as part of your mindfulness practice, take careful note of the way that you and your friends and colleagues speak about foreigners. Apply some of the insights you gained during the eighth step to these discussions. Listen critically to the voices in your own society that preach hatred or disdain of other national, religious, and cultural traditions. Is there not something disturbingly familiar about it? Do you hear the hauteur of the colonialist or the bigotry of the fascist in some of their arguments? A dehumanizing discourse that seeks to dominate a group often uses the language of disgust and contempt: this kind of thinking led to the enslavement and oppression of African and Native Americans, the Armenian genocide, the Shoah, apartheid in South Africa, the tribal wars in Rwanda, and the mass killings in Bosnia.

When you read the newspaper or watch the news, take note of the way the Four Fs, often cloaked in high-minded, patriotic, or religious rhetoric, still dominate public affairs and human behavior. They are not confined to the fundamentalist or conservative camp, but can also be detected in some so-called liberal discourse. How often do you hear the "principle of charity" at work? Despite our advanced civilization and sophistication, to what extent are we still prey to the mechanisms of the me-first old brain? When you defend something you feel tribal about, take note of the way your threat mechanism has been activated, so that you lose your dispassion and ability to assess the other side fairly and rationally. Notice the way you become "puffed up" with righteous aggression, your anger, disgust, and desire to wound. Do you sense in yourself, or in your friends and fellow countrymen, a tendency to follow the leader blindly during a political, cultural, or social crisis so that you cry, in effect, "My country, right or wrong"?

Recall the seventh step: How Little We Know. How much of the confident talk you hear about the backwardness, arrogance, or intolerance of other national, cultural, ethnic, or religious groups is based purely on hearsay? When you or your friends are critical of another nation, how much do you actually know about it? Make a list of what you know for certain about its history, its culture, and its current circumstances. How reliable are your sources? If you feel incensed when people attack your own cultural or religious values, is it ethical to inflict that pain on others? Consider Jesus's words: "Why do you observe the splinter in your brother's eye and never notice the plank in your own? How dare you say to your brother: 'let me take the splinter out of your eye,' when all the time there is a plank in your own? Hypocrite! Take the plank out of your own eye first, and then you will see clearly enough to take the splinter out of your brother's eye."[5]

Do we hear enough international news in the media? Are conflicts in other regions reported objectively and their background explained? Do you get to hear both sides of a dispute, or is reporting based on a narrowly national agenda? If you work in the media, consider how we can learn about the plight of our neighbors and adjust to the realities of our global society. Educators should realize that they have a responsibility to make sure that our children are given accurate, balanced, and respectful information about other peoples. If this had been done more carefully in the past, perhaps we would not be having so many problems in the present.

We have thought carefully about the way our own suffering affects the way we behave. We have learned that the seeds of our anger are often in our own minds and that it is neither helpful nor accurate to assume that other people are always responsible for our pain. When you see violence in other parts of the world portrayed on the evening news, do you look askance at the rage and hatred in people's faces, or do you ask yourself about the distress that has inspired this anger? Make a habit of looking behind the headlines to the ordinary people who are affected by a crisis. Remember that they did not choose to be born into that part of the world. Like you, they simply found themselves in a particular situation and may have been forced to conduct their whole lives in a context of violence, deprivation, and despair.

We know from our own experience that deeds have long-term consequences. We are all affected, consciously and unconsciously, by the unkindness, neglect, contempt, and violence we have endured in the past. This is also true of whole nations: persecution, chronic warfare, bad governance, exploitation, marginalization, occupation, humiliation, enslavement, exile, impoverishment, and defamation all leave psychic scars that persist long after the event. They affect the way the new generation is brought up and can infiltrate the religious, intellectual, ethical, and social development of a country. People who have been taught to despise themselves cannot easily respect others. Those who have been brutalized by hatred, persecution, or oppression cannot readily cultivate the trust that makes it possible to reach out to others. We should ask whether our own nation has contributed to the problems of a particular region and realize that, in our global world, if we ignore the pain of a people, it is likely that at some point this negligence will rebound on us.

Remember Confucius's advice about the way to apply the ethic of the Golden Rule to politics: "You yourself desire rank and standing; then help others to get rank and standing. You want to turn your merits to account; then help others to turn theirs to account."[6] We can no longer thrive at the expense of others. A practically expressed respect for the other is probably indispensable for a peaceful global society.

During this step, incorporate a new Buddhist exercise into your mindfulness practice. It will help you to appreciate how dependent you are on people you have never met and who may live far away. As you walk around your home, bring to mind all the people who built it, treated its timbers, baked its bricks, installed the plumbing, and wove your linens. When you get up in the morning, remember those who planted, picked, and spun the cotton of your sheets and who collected, treated, and exported the beans you grind for your morning coffee. You enjoy their products, so you have a responsibility for them, especially if they were working in poor conditions. Who baked the bread you toast for breakfast? Become aware of the labor that went into the production of each slice. As you set off to work, reflect on the thousands of workers and engineers who build and maintain the roads, cars, railroads, planes, trains, and underground transport on which you rely. Continue this exercise throughout the day. We should also make ourselves aware that our cultural, ethical, religious, and intellectual traditions have all been profoundly affected by other peoples'. We think of them as ours, but they may in the past have been deeply influenced by the ancestors of those we now regard as enemies. We are what we are because of the hard work, insights, and achievements of countless others.

When we are braced defensively to withstand a threat, we cannot think intelligently or creatively. If we allow ourselves to feel anger or disdain, this will affect our spiritual and intellectual health, because ingratitude and hatred shrink our horizons. Zhuangzi would say that it is unrealistic to try to freeze our cultural, national, or religious traditions in their current mode. Think of how radically they have changed and adapted to new conditions over the centuries and even within your lifetime. The meditation on the Immeasurables is designed precisely to bring down the barriers we erect against the other so that our horizons can expand.

Letting go of our "tribal" egotism can become a spiritual process, which is beautifully illustrated in the story of the Prophet Muhammad's Night Journey (*isrā'*) to Jerusalem and his Ascension to Heaven (*mi'rāj*).[7] This is a mythos; it describes an archetypal process rather than an accurate occurrence. There are references in the Qur'an to a mystical

experience of the Prophet, but they don't resemble the de-
tailed narrative that was written down for the first time
during the eighth century.[8] Muhammad's early biogra-
phers inserted the story into the period when the Prophet
was being forced to leave Mecca, abandon his tribe, and
take up permanent residence with another, and like any
myth, it explores the deeper significance of what was hap-
pening. The *hijrah* ("migration") from Mecca to the agricul-
tural settlement of Medina, some 250 miles to the north,
was more than a change of address: abandoning your tribe,
the most sacred value of all, amounted to blasphemy in
Arabia at this time. The word *hijrah* itself suggests a painful rupture, its root *HJR* meaning "he cut himself off from
friendly or loving communication or intercourse . . . he
ceased . . . to associate with them."[9]

Traditional Arab odes often depicted the poet embark-
ing on a night journey, a terrifying trek across the desert,
before enjoying a joyful reunion with his tribe, which he
celebrates in a hymn of praise to its unique superiority, its
valor in war, and its eternal hatred of those who threaten
its survival.[10] But Muhammad's Night Journey reverses
this pattern. Instead of ending in a tribal reunion, the
journey finishes in faraway Jerusalem, the holy city of
Jews and Christians. Instead of glorifying hatred and war,
it is a story of harmony and transcendence of the tribal
group. One night, so the story goes, when Muhammad was
sleeping beside the Kabah, he was awakened by Gabriel,
the spirit of revelation, and miraculously conveyed to the
Temple Mount in Jerusalem. There he was greeted by all
the great prophets of the past, who invited him to preach

to them before he began his ascent, like a Jewish mystic, through the seven heavens to the throne of God. The story falls reverently silent when Muhammad enters the divine presence, but it is clear that it was based on the surrender (*islam*) of the ego: "In awe, he lost his speech and lost himself—Muhammad did not know Muhammad here, saw not himself."[11]

The mythos is an expression of the Prophet's yearning to bring the Arabs, who had long felt that they were off the map of the divine plan, into the heart of the monotheistic family. Instead of shunning the newcomer as a pretender, the other prophets welcome him as a brother. At each stage of his journey through the seven heavens, Muhammad meets and talks with Adam, Jesus, John the Baptist, Joseph, Enoch, Moses, Aaron, and Abraham. In one version of the story, Moses gives him advice about the number of times that Muslims should pray each day. It is a story of pluralism: the prophets pray together, embrace one another, and share their insights. It has become a paradigm of authentic Muslim spirituality, representing the perfect "surrender" of both the personal and the tribal ego.

The Sufis, the mystics of Islam, who have a particular devotion to this story, developed an outstanding appreciation of other faiths. It is quite common for a Sufi poet to cry in ecstasy that he is no longer a Jew, a Christian, or a Muslim and is equally at home in a synagogue, mosque, temple, or church, because once you have glimpsed the divine, you have left these man-made distinctions behind. As we leave this step, we should meditate on the words of the influential Sufi philosopher Muid ad-Din ibn al-Arabi (1165–1240). His warning against religious exclusivity can also be applied to any "tribal" chauvinism.

> Do not attach yourself to any particular creed so exclusively that you disbelieve all the rest; otherwise you will lose much good, nay, you will fail to recognize the real truth of the matter. God, the omnipresent and omnipotent, is not limited by any one creed, for, he says, "Wheresoever ye turn, there is the face of Allah."[12] Everyone praises what he believes; his god is his own creature, and in praising it he praises himself. Consequently he blames the beliefs of others, which he would not do if he were just, but his dislike is based on ignorance.[13]

In the next step, we shall try correct this ignorance.

Knowledge

We have considered the importance of abandoning a tribal outlook in order to "get to know one another." But this is not easy. We all have busy lives, and not everybody has either the time or the inclination to undertake the difficult and sensitive task of deciphering the cultural, religious, and political customs of other peoples. We need the help of experts, and most of us rely on the media or our governments for this kind of information. Yet those who live in a democracy may find themselves voting for politicians who have a partial or even tribal worldview. We owe it to our own nation and to others to develop a wider, more panoptic knowledge and understanding of our neighbors.

First, recall the seventh step and remind yourself yet again of how little we know. People often pontificate about foreign affairs from a position of dangerous ignorance. The media are not always reliable: some newspapers or television channels have political or social agendas that slant their coverage of world events. The same is often true of politicians. In Britain during the buildup to the Iraq war, the government told the public that Saddam Hussein had weapons of mass destruction that he could use to attack British bases in Cyprus at forty minutes' notice. Later it transpired that this was not the case. Many of the people who believed in the war were unaware that Western governments had supported and armed Saddam for years and therefore bore a measure of responsibility for the suffering he had inflicted on his people. The effort of getting to know one another demands sound information and a willingness to question received ideas. We may not have Socrates to goad us into self-knowledge and an appreciation of the profundity of our ignorance, but we can make a serious effort to fill in some of the gaps in our knowledge. If you belong to a reading discussion group, you could use it to study books and articles that challenge some preconceived notions and discuss your reactions.

Again, we begin with ourselves. We often have a myopic view of the history of our own country or religious tradition and criticize others for behavior of which "we" have been guilty in the past or even continue to be in the present. After the atrocities of September 11, 2001, I was often taken aback by the way some Christians berated the violence and intolerance they attributed to Islam, showing not only an embarrassing ignorance of Muslim history but a surprising blindness to the crusades, inquisitions, persecutions, and wars of religion that had scarred their own faith. I often felt that alongside programs titled "Understanding Islam" there should be a parallel course called "Understanding Christianity." There was also a worrying lack of awareness about Western behavior during the colonial era, which had contributed to some of our current problems. A double standard, albeit unintended, violates our integrity and damages our credibility. In a global society, conflict is rarely the fault of only one party. All participants in a conflict have sown bad karma in the past, and we are all now reaping the results.

When we are about to criticize another nation or religious tradition, we should get into the habit of catching ourselves and asking whether our own country may have been responsible for a similar abuse in the past. An instinctive, tribal response that leaps to the defense of the leader, whatever the rights and wrongs of the situation, can no longer suffice. Building on our reflections during the second step, we need to stand back critically and adopt a more impartial attitude. In the meditation on the Immeasurables, we have been trying to cultivate the equanimity that is essential to the compassionate life. The Sanskrit *upeksha* ("even-mindedness") derives from *upa* ("over") and *iksh* ("to look"). As we develop "concern for everybody," we are seeking a more objective overview that sees the situation as a whole. *Upeksha* presupposes an awareness of prejudices, preconceptions, attachments, and blind spots that can cloud our understanding. We are striving for an equability that can look at world problems without undue attachment to our national self-interest and that can transcend religious or cultural chauvinism in an appreciation of others.

We cannot instantly become masters of world, religious, and cultural history. Instead, it is better to concentrate our efforts initially on getting to know just one or two of our global neighbors. During this step, two exercises will help you to expand your sympathies. First, choose a foreign country that you find attractive. It may be one that you enjoy visiting and know quite well, or if you have not had much opportunity to travel, choose a country that has intrigued you. Instead of another nation, you might prefer to look at a religious or cultural tradition other than your own. The point is that you will now be activating an interest in the "stranger." Once or twice a month make a point of reading an article or a novel or watching a movie about the stranger you have chosen, so that it becomes a vivid and regular presence in your life. Ask yourself what this foreign national or religious tradition can teach you. Are there things that they do better than we do? Have they influenced us in the past? What do you think that we could teach them?

Your investigations should not be a dreary duty. You can make them fun. Try to find out more about this country's poetry and literature. Try learning the language. Listen to the music of the people you have chosen, experiment with their cuisine, start following the national soccer team, and invite friends to join you in a celebration of its national holidays. If you have chosen to study another religion, attend a worship service, and if you have friends who belong to this tradition, ask them to help you. Perhaps they will invite you to a seder, Eid, or Diwali. When Wilfred Cantwell Smith (1916–2000), the distinguished Canadian scholar of comparative religion, was teaching Islamic studies at McGill University, he used to make his students observe the fast during Ramadan, celebrate Islamic holidays, and perform the prayers at the correct times—even get up for the dawn prayer—because he was convinced that it was impossible to understand another faith simply by reading books about it.

Look into the history of the country or religious tradition you have chosen and find out more about its triumphs or failures. Look out for any mention of it in the news. You might find it helpful to consult a website, such as Search for Common Ground (www.sfcg.org), which gives regular updates on different countries, or subscribe to a periodical dealing with foreign affairs. The object of the exercise is "to make room for the other" in your mind. You will need to approach it with the "science of compassion." When you come up against something difficult, keep on asking "But why?" Keep trying to understand the entire context of an event, pushing your mind forward so that you can imagine yourself in similar circumstances feeling the same way. Getting to know other peoples and traditions is not easy. There will always be things that we do not understand or find difficult to appreciate—just as we are sometimes puzzled by the behavior of our closest friends—but to experience the limits of our understanding, realizing how little we *can* know is itself a valuable experience.

As you progress, you will probably become aware that

everything is more complex than you thought. We tend to see other peoples in simplified snapshots similar to the sound bites of the evening news that stick stubbornly in our minds. People often assume, for example, that London is perpetually shrouded in fog, because they have seen too many television adaptations of Charles Dickens, and that it is always raining, even though London actually has less rainfall per year than Rome, Istanbul, or Sydney (though I fully admit most of it does fall in summer!). People also seem to think that Britons drink gallons of tea every day and reel back in astonishment when I refuse a cup— I have disliked the stuff all my life! As you get to know your "adopted" country or tradition a little better, you will begin to notice this stereotypical thinking in your friends and will want to put them right. You may also find that they are surprisingly resistant to changing their perceptions and ideas, because these have become part of their private geography.

When you make the meditation on the Immeasurables, you might include the people you are getting to know, extending to them your friendship, compassion, sympathetic joy, and equanimity. Think of the marvelous qualities of the country or tradition you are studying, feel gratitude for its particular contribution to humanity, but also recall its suffering, its failures, and its crimes, and extend your compassion to it. Remember the millions of people who have participated in this tradition or been citizens of this country, each with their own history of pain, and wish for them everything that you wish for yourself. Finally, you will regard them with *upeksha:* their traditions may be as flawed as your own, yet you extend your compassion, friendship, and sympathetic joy to them nonetheless.

Once you have begun to appreciate the complexity of understanding another country or tradition, it is time to embark on the second exercise of this step. Here you will be investigating issues that are more sensitive. Turn to the Suggestions for Further Reading and find the section headed Concern for Everybody. Here I have listed some books about the current tension between the West and the Islamic world, a topic of major concern at the moment and one on which most people have an opinion. First read the titles and get a sense of the range of issues that are being discussed. Then select a book that you think will reflect your point of view and another that will probably challenge it. Here too you will need to apply the "science of compassion" and the "principle of charity." Again, remember the seventh step: How Little We Know. As you read, list the ways in which both authors have altered your thinking.

Do not leave this tenth step until you feel that you are beginning to change your mind. This does not mean that you should reverse all your former opinions; rather, you will be developing a healthy distrust of what the Buddha called hearsay. During this step, you will have been engaging in a Socratic dialogue with yourself, overcoming the limitations of the unexamined life and the dangers of habitual tribal thinking

As you get ready to take the next step, you might like to include this very early Buddhist poem in your daily routine. It is a marvelous conclusion to the Immeasurables:

*Let all beings be happy! Weak or strong, of high, middle
or low estate, small or great, visible or invisible, near
or far away, alive or still to be born—May they all be
perfectly happy!*

*Let nobody lie to anybody or despise any single being
anywhere.*

*May nobody wish harm to any single creature out of
anger or hatred!*

Let us cherish all creatures, as a mother her only child!

*May our loving thoughts fill the whole world, above,
below, across—without limit; our love will know no
obstacles—a boundless goodwill toward the whole
world, unrestricted, free of hatred or enmity.*

*Whether we are standing or walking, sitting or lying
down, as long as we are awake we should cultivate
this love in our heart. This is the noblest way of
living.*[1]

Recognition

At a very unhappy period of her life, Christina Noble had a powerful dream: "Naked children were running down a dirt road fleeing from a napalm bombing . . . one of the girls had a look in her eyes that implored me to pick her up and protect her and take her to safety. Above the escaping children was a brilliant white light that contained the word 'Vietnam.'"[1] From that moment, Christina was convinced, in a way she could not understand, that it was her destiny to go to Vietnam and that one day she would work with children there.

It is not difficult to see why this dream made such an impression on her. Forty years later, the memory of her own childhood still makes her voice "high and tight, and there is a hint of fear."[2] At the age of twelve, she had become a child of the streets in Dublin, sleeping in public toilets during the winter and under the bushes of Phoenix Park in the summer. She was perpetually hungry: a priest once discovered her eating wax drippings from the votive candles in front of a statue of Christ and threw her out of the church. One night she was raped by two men, and when they dropped her back on the streets, torn, bleeding, her face bruised and swollen, she was struck by "the horrible realization that there was nobody for me to go to. I needed just one person who would not see me as dust, or barely more than an animal."[3] One of the men had made her pregnant: Christina was placed in a harsh institution, the child was taken from her, and she eventually stowed away on a boat that took her to England, where she married a Greek named Mario who abused her but who gave her three children. It was during this time that she had her dream.

Christina's life changed for the better when she left Mario and with the help of her new partner started a successful catering company. But she never wavered in her belief that she was destined to work with children in Vietnam. In 1989 she felt that the time had come and made her first visit to the country. One day, while she was watching two destitute little girls playing in the dirt of the street, one of them smiled at her and tried to hold her hand. Christina was immediately overcome with memories so painful that she tried to walk away; she wanted no more grief, no more involvement. Yet all the time she was saying to herself: "There's no difference between an Irish gutter and a Vietnamese gutter. At the end of the day they are the same." Suddenly past and present came together, and Christina realized that the Vietnamese girl was the child she had seen so long ago in her dream. Sobbing, she sank down in the dirt and pulled the children into her lap, promising to take care of them. This was a major turning point: "Here the pain, sorrow and anger of my childhood in Ireland would be resolved. I would work with the street children of Ho Chi Minh City. Here I would stay. Here I would find happiness."[4]

Christina became a crusader for the street children of Vietnam. She founded an orphanage with the help of wealthy businessmen, and later established the Christina Noble Children's Foundation in London, which raised thousands of dollars. This enabled her to open the Children's Medical and Social Centre in Ho Chi Minh City in 1991, just two years after her first visit to the country. There are now foundations in France, the United States, and Australia. When she began her work, friends told her that she was attempting the impossible. "You are only one person," they insisted. But Christina never forgot that "when I was a child, I needed only one person to understand my suffering and pain. . . . One is very important."[5] Her life has been a demonstration of this truth.

Let us consider the moment of recognition. When Christina looked into the child's face, she saw herself; she realized that there was no "us" and "them"; "at the end of the day they are the same." From a purely rational perspective, this statement makes little sense. There must be a thousand differences between a Vietnamese and an Irish gutter; surely it would have made more sense for Christina to work for homeless children in Ireland; there was no *real* connection between herself and the Vietnamese girl.

But during the previous steps, we have been developing a more empathetic outlook, based on imagination rather than logic. Our work has revealed that we are not alone in our suffering but that everybody is in pain. Instead of retreating into the Buddha's pleasure park, we have allowed our own unhappiness and the sorrow of other people to invade our consciousness. We have learned that we cannot put ourselves in a special, separate category. Instead we have tried to cultivate the considerate attitude of *shu* ("likening to oneself"), reflexively relating our own pain to the distress of others. As a result, we are beginning to acquire what Tibetan Buddhists call "the inability to bear the sight of another's sorrow," so that we feel it almost as intensely as we feel our own.

We are probably deluged with more images of pain than any previous generation; they are beamed into our homes nightly on the evening news. It is easy to get compassion fatigue and tempting to dismiss these spectacles from our minds, telling ourselves that there is nothing we personally can do and that this misery has nothing to do with us. Christina had probably seen and subliminally remembered the famous television footage of the little Vietnamese girl running in terror from a napalm bombing; it was an image that probably did more than any political speech to turn American public opinion against the Vietnam War. She could easily have thrust it from her mind, telling herself that she had, after all, suffered enough. But she had unconsciously made the connection between herself and the Vietnamese child. She did not allow herself to forget her dream—as if she knew at some subconscious level that it was the clue that would one day bring her out of her own labyrinth.

Her story suggests how we too can achieve a similar moment of recognition. Instead of steeling ourselves against the intrusion of other people's pain, we should regard our exposure to global suffering as a spiritual opportunity. Make a conscious effort to allow these television images to enter your consciousness and take up residence there. Extend your hospitality to them, and "make place for the other" in your life. It is a powerful way of developing "concern for everybody." If a particular image speaks to you strongly, focus on it as Christina did. As in her case, there may be a special reason for this. Bring this image deliberately to mind at various times in the day. Summon it when you are feeling sorry for yourself—or during a moment of happiness, when you are filled with gratitude for your good fortune. Make a friend of the distressed person, so that she becomes a presence in your life: direct your thoughts of loving kindness and compassion to her during your meditation on the Immeasurables.

But it cannot stop there. Christina found that the way to transcend the overwhelming memories of her appalling childhood was to work practically to alleviate the pain of others. If we hug the memory of our own grief to ourselves, we can close our minds to other people's wretchedness. We may even think that our unhappy experiences give us special privileges. But the Golden Rule requires us to use our afflictions to make a difference in the lives of others. We cannot allow ourselves to feel paralyzed by the immensity of global misery. Christina's story reminds us of the significant difference that one person can make.

We cannot all rush off to foreign parts as Christina did. Indeed, there is no need to do so: we will find plenty of opportunities on our own doorstep. Suffering is not confined to distant parts of the globe. During this step, take time to look around your world again. Your training in mindfulness and new appreciation of the ubiquity of pain should make you experience your immediate environment differently. You may find that you are now more sensitized to the sorrow that is present wherever we look. We need to train our minds to *see* it. Because we have a self-protective tendency to keep suffering at bay, insulating ourselves in a psychological equivalent of the Buddha's pleasure park, we sometimes fail to recognize the signs of poverty, loneliness, grief, fear, and desolation in our own city, our own village, or our own family. So look at your world anew, and do not leave this step until you have chosen your mission. There is a need that you—and only you—can fulfill. Do not imagine that you are doomed to a life of grim austerity or that your involvement in suffering will drain your life of fun. In fact, you may find that alleviating the distress of others makes you a good deal happier. Journalists often compare Christina to the late Mother Teresa, but she will have none of it.

I don't know why they do that, it only proves they don't really know me. I do all the things a saint wouldn't do. I belt out songs in clubs . . . I enjoy a double whisky now and then. I love dancing. I like to ride fast on the back of a Honda. Although I detest violence if I have to protect a child by giving someone a wallop, I'll do it. I'm more than a bit wild. I'm Irish. Mother Teresa I am not.[6]

Reaching out generously to embrace the pain of another yields an *ekstasis,* because in such a moment we are leaving our egotistic selves behind. This is beautifully illustrated by the following three biblical myths, which all center on a moment of recognition. Remember that a myth is a program for action: you will recognize its truth only when you put it into practice in your own life.

First, let us look at this very ancient story of Abraham. Later Jews would vigorously deny that it was possible to see God, and yet the biblical author tells us that

> Yahweh appeared to [Abraham] at the Oak of Mamre while he was sitting by the entrance to his tent during the hottest part of the day. He looked up, and there he saw three men standing near him. As soon as he saw them he ran from the entrance of the tent to meet them, and bowed to the ground. "My lord," he said, "I beg you, if I find favour with you, kindly do not pass your servant by. A little water shall be brought; you shall wash your feet and lie down under the tree. Let me fetch a little bread and you shall refresh yourselves before going any further. That is why you have come in your servant's direction." They replied, "Do as you say."

Abraham hastened to the tent to find Sarah. "Hurry," he said, "knead three bushels of flour and make loaves." Then running to the cattle Abraham took a fine and tender calf and gave it to the servant, who hurried to prepare it. Then taking cream, milk and the calf he had prepared, he laid it all before them, and they ate while he remained standing near them under the tree.[7]

In the ancient world, foreigners were dangerous; because they were not bound by the local vendetta, they could kill and plunder with impunity. Even today, very few of us would willingly bring three total strangers off the street into our own homes. But Abraham shows no such reluctance. On the contrary, he rushes out to greet the travelers, prostrates himself before them as if they were gods or kings, brings them into his encampment, and gives them the best of what he has. This practical act of compassion leads to a divine encounter.

There is no crude moment of revelation; Yahweh does not suddenly unmask himself. It simply emerges in the narrative, without any fanfare, that God is somehow present in this meeting and mysteriously takes part in the ensuing conversation. He seems to speak through the three strangers. They ask Abraham where his wife Sarah is, and one of them promises: "I shall visit you again next year without fail and your wife will then have a son." Sarah, who is eavesdropping, laughs at the absurdity of this prediction, because she is a very old woman. Suddenly it transpires, though, that the stranger *is* Yahweh:

But Yahweh asked Abraham, "Why did Sarah laugh and say, 'Am I really going to have a child now that I am old?' Is anything too wonderful for Yahweh: At the same time next year, I shall visit you again, and Sarah will have a son."[8]

Yet when the strangers leave, "Abraham remained standing before Yahweh."[9] Instead of thinking that the plight of these passing travelers has nothing to do with him, Abraham has "made place for the other" in his life. He has thrown down the precautionary barriers we erect to protect ourselves from harm and entered a sacred dimension of experience. In Hebrew, the world for "holiness" is *qaddosh,* which literally means "separate, other." This myth suggests that if instead of excluding the stranger we welcome him, overcoming our inertia, reluctance, fear, or initial repugnance, we will have intimations of the transcendent Otherness that some call "God."

There is a similar moment in the New Testament in Saint Luke's gospel. It is three days after Jesus's crucifixion, and two of his disciples are walking together from Jerusalem to nearby Emmaus.[10] They are naturally in great distress. On the road, they fall in with another traveler, who asks them why they are so troubled. Instead of telling him to mind his own business, they share with him the terrible story of Jesus's execution, explaining that they had believed he was the Messiah. The disciples are taking a risk, because the stranger could easily have ridiculed them. But they have the courage to open their hearts to him, expose their raw vulnerability, and confide their most intimate hopes

to somebody they have never met before. Their trust is re-
warded. Instead of jeering at them, the stranger is able to
comfort them. Starting with Moses, he begins to expound
the "full message of the prophets," arguing that the Messiah was destined to suffer before entering his glory. In
fact, there is nothing in either the Torah or the prophetic
writings to suggest any such thing. The stranger has em-
barked on some highly inventive rabbinic midrash, and
the disciples could have rebuked him for taking too many
liberties with the original texts and dismissed his exegesis
as nonsense. But again, they are ready to listen to his insights; they allow him to change their minds about their
own faith, which is enhanced by this input. Later they
would remember how their hearts "burned within them"
when the stranger expounded the scriptures.

It is another story of hospitality: the disciples have allowed a stranger to enter their minds and have let his
ideas find a home there. When they arrive at their destina-
tion, the disciples beg their new friend to stay the night
with them. The moment of recognition comes when the
stranger breaks bread at dinner, and they understand that
all the time they have been in the presence of the Messiah,
the *christos*, but that their "eyes had been held" from realizing it. It is only a fleeting illumination: almost immediately
he vanishes from their sight. Henceforth, Luke suggests,
Christians will glimpse the risen Christ only in the Eucha-
rist, in the study of scripture—and when they reach out to
the stranger. We may find that if instead of retreating from
the stranger and rejecting his insights out of hand, we allow him to change our perceptions, our understanding of

our own traditions may be enriched by the encounter and we too may have moments of numinous insight.

Finally, consider the famous story of Yaakov (in English we call him Jacob) wrestling with a mysterious stranger on his return to Canaan. Twenty years earlier, after gravely wronging his twin brother, Esau, Yaakov had fled for his life to Mesopotamia. Now he is returning with his family to the Promised Land and is very apprehensive about seeing Esau again. When he hears that his brother is coming to meet him with a company of four hundred men, Yaakov is terrified. He sends his family across the Jordan River ahead of him and dispatches servants to Esau with a generous gift of livestock, saying to himself: "I will wipe [the anger from] his face with the gift that goes ahead of my face; afterward when I see his face, perhaps he will lift up my face!"[11]

Then Yaakov is left alone.

Now a man wrestled with him until the coming up at dawn. When he saw that he could not prevail against him, he touched the socket of his thigh; the socket of Yaakov's thigh had been dislocated as he wrestled with him. Then he said: Let me go, for dawn has come up! But he said: I will not let you go unless you bless me. He said to him: What is your name? And he said: Yaakov. Then he said: Not as Yaakov shall your name be henceforth uttered, but rather as Yisrael ["God Fighter"], for you have fought with God and men and have prevailed. Then Yaakov asked and said: Pray tell me your name! But he said: Now why do you ask after my name? And he gave him farewell-blessing there.

Yaakov called the name of the place: Peniel ["Face of God"], for I have seen God face to face, he said, and my life has been saved. The sun rose on him as he crossed by Peniel and he was limping on his thigh.[12]

The story reads like a dream in which we confront issues that we suppress in our waking lives. The wrestling match recalls the struggle Yaakov and Esau had in their mother's womb when they had "almost crushed one another inside her."[13] When the twins finally came to birth, Yaakov ("Heel Holder"), the second born, was grasping his brother's heel. In mythology, twins often represent two halves of a single whole: Esau is his alter ego, and yet Yaakov has been fighting with him all his life. Yaakov and Esau also represent two nations—Israel and Edom—who are locked in perpetual conflict.[14] As he wrestles with the stranger, Yaakov is fighting with his brother, his God, and himself. Notice how the text makes it difficult to distinguish between Yaakov and the stranger, and how it repeatedly applies the word "face" to Yaakov, Esau, and God in a way that merges them in the reader's mind.

Enmity shapes our consciousness and identity. The people we hate haunt us; they inhabit our minds in a negative way as we brood in a deviant form of meditation on their bad qualities. The enemy thus becomes our twin, a shadow self whom we come to resemble. Like Yaakov, nations may also feel deep antagonism toward people they have wronged, and the enemy may become so central to national consciousness and identity that he becomes a second self. If we want to achieve reconciliation, not only do we have to struggle with the enemy, but we also have to wrestle with ourselves. And in the struggle, this myth tells us, we may find ourselves blessed and embraced by the presence of something greater. The next day when the brothers meet, Esau behaves with the magnanimity of a young prince, running toward his twin and embracing him. The two men weep together: like the Greeks, they feel that the sorrow of their shared past has created a bond between them. It is a moment of *shalom,* of "peace, wholeness, and completion." Yaakov at once connects this *ekstasis* of reconciliation with the epiphany of Peniel, telling Esau, "For I have, after all, seen your face, as one sees the face of God, and you have been gracious to me."[15]

We are nearing the end of our journey. As we prepare to take the final step, we should think of Yaakov after his bruising struggle with the stranger. Although wounded by the encounter, he has been blessed by his assailant and is walking toward his erstwhile enemy in the light of a new day.

Love Your Enemies

The Golden Rule teaches that "I" value my own self and my own tribe and nation as much as you do yours. The great sages who formulated it believed that if "I" made my personal and political identity and survival an absolute value, human society would be impossible, so they urged us all to "yield" to one another. We have seen that many of these prophets, mystics, and sages were living in a time when violence had risen to new heights and when the infant market economy was fostering rapacious greed. The primitive emotions of the reptilian brain had been made more powerful by the new brain ability of *Homo sapiens* to reason, calculate, and invent technology that had enhanced his powers. At the beginning of the Warring States period, Mozi tried to persuade the princes of his day that "concern for everybody" made good practical sense and would be in their best interest—an insight that has become even more pertinent today. We recall the Dalai Lama's suggestion that the concept of war has become outdated. Warfare is an integral part of human history, but it no longer makes sense in our global society. If we destroy our neighbors or ignore their interests, this will eventually rebound hideously back on ourselves.[1]

During the third century BCE, shortly before the terrible conclusion of the Warring States era, the anonymous Chinese author we know as Laozi pointed out that no matter how good his intentions, violence always recoils upon the perpetrator. You cannot force people to behave as you wish; coercive methods are more likely to drive them to the exact opposite. The *Daodejing* is usually read today as a devotional text, but it was in fact a manual of statecraft, written for the ruler of one of the small principalities that was about to be destroyed by the large state of Qin. The text offers the vulnerable prince, who is haunted by the terror of imminent annihilation, a survival strategy. In political life, Laozi argues, people always prefer to engage in furious activity and a massive show of strength, but force and coercion are self-destructive. Everything that goes up must come down: that is a law of life, so to strengthen your enemy by yielding to him would actually hasten his decline.

The wise ruler realizes that "arms are ill-omened instruments" and uses them "only when he cannot do otherwise."[2] Laozi was not a pacifist; he believed that sometimes war was a regrettable necessity. But he did advocate an attitude of restrained aggression that would prevent the escalation of hatred and violence:

The good leader in war is not warlike
The good fighter is not impetuous;
The best conqueror of the enemy is he who never takes
the offensive.
The man who gets the most out of men is the one who
treats them with humility.[3]

Tyrants cause their own downfall, because when a prince tries to impose his will on other people, they automatically resist him, so a sagacious prince would resort to arms only with regret and as a last resort. There must be no triumphalism, chauvinism, or aggressive patriotism: he knows that he must bring hostilities to an end gently. "Bring it to a conclusion, but do not boast; bring it to a conclusion, but do not brag; bring it to a conclusion, but do not be arrogant; bring it to a conclusion, but only where there is no choice; bring it to a conclusion, but do not intimidate."[4]

Such an attitude was possible only if the ruler trained his mind and became a sage; he had to discipline the me-first aggression that is our instinctive response to any threat. As a first step, he must learn to appreciate the inadequacy of language and realize that true insight does not consist of the acquisition of information but comes from mastering our egotism and greed.[5] A sage-ruler does not pontificate about his principles; he does not try to make the people what *he* wants them to be, but "takes as his own mind the mind of the people."[6] The only person who is fit to rule is the man who has overcome the habit of selfishness:

The reason there is great affliction is that I have a self.
If I had no self, what affliction would I have?
Therefore to one who honours the world as his self
The world may be entrusted,
And to one who loves the world as one's self
The world may be consigned.[7]

It was not a sage-king who emerged victorious at the end of the Warring States period but the ruthlessly aggressive state of Qin, which destroyed all the remaining states and established its empire in 221 BCE. However, Laozi was proved right in the end, because Qin's cruel, oppressive policies led to a popular rebellion in 209 that brought the dynasty to a premature end.

We can stop the vicious cycle of attack and counter-attack, strike and counterstrike that holds the world in thrall today only if we learn to appreciate the wisdom of restraint toward the enemy. We have seen that when Jesus told his followers to love their enemies, he also urged an ethic of *ahimsa*. The written Torah permitted limited retaliation, so you could take *only* an eye for an eye or a tooth for a tooth[8]—but as Gandhi famously remarked, "An eye for an eye makes the whole world blind": Jesus was asking us to show courage when he told his disciples, "Offer the wicked man no resistance."[9]

But I say this to you who are listening: Love your enemies, do good to those who hate you, bless those who curse you, pray for those who treat you badly. To the man who slaps you on one cheek, present the other cheek too; to the man who takes your cloak from you, do not refuse your tunic. Give to everyone who asks you, and do not ask for your property back from the man who robs you. Treat others as you would like them to treat you.[10]

Jesus is preaching an openhanded, openhearted attitude designed, as in the *Daodejing,* to disarm the enemy. Such love expects no personal recompense. "If you love those who love you, what thanks can you expect? . . . Instead, love your enemies and do good, and lend without any hope of return."[11] The Greek text is obscure here: the last phrase could also mean "driving no one to despair" or "despairing of no one." We have witnessed the result of hard-line policies inspired by a righteousness that can see only the worst in the enemy. We have seen the danger of ruthless retaliation that drives people to despair, ignores their needs, and refuses to take their aspirations seriously. We have become aware that when people feel that they have nothing to lose, they resort to hopeless, self-destructive measures.

This voice of compassion is not confined to the distant past. We have heard it in recent times. At the end of his life, Gandhi claimed that he no longer hated anybody. He might hate the oppressive system of British colonialism, but he could not hate the people who implemented it. "Mine is not an exclusive love. I cannot love Moslems or Hindus and hate Englishmen. For if I love merely Hindus and Moslems because their ways are on the whole pleasing to me, I shall soon begin to hate them when their ways displease me, as they may well do any moment. A love that is based on the goodness of those whom you love is a mercenary affair."[12] Without any feelings of recrimination, Nelson Mandela walked out of the South African prison in which he had been confined for twenty-seven years, and when he came to power initiated a process of reconciliation rather than seeking revenge. The Dalai Lama was exiled from Tibet by the Chinese as a young man, and although he saw his monasteries destroyed and his monks massacred, he has persistently refused to condemn the Chinese.

Martin Luther King Jr. believed that the highest point of Jesus's life was the moment when he forgave his executioners, when instead of attempting to defeat evil with evil, he was able to prevail over it with good: "Only goodness can drive out evil and only love can overcome hate."[13] Loving our enemies means that we have to accept "the necessity, over and over again, of forgiving those who inflict evil and injury on us." King was convinced that this was "an absolute necessity for our survival . . . the key to the solution of the problems of our world."[14] We could not allow the injury our enemies inflict upon us to become an insuperable barrier to a more positive relationship. "We must not seek to defeat or humiliate the enemy but to win his friendship and understanding," King insisted. "Every word and deed must contribute to an understanding with the enemy and release those vast reservoirs of goodwill which have been blocked by the impenetrable walls of hate."[15]

But compassion involves risk and makes us vulnerable: King was assassinated in 1968. He knew that hatred was inspired by fear but always remained convinced that only love could cure this "disease": "Hatred paralyzes life; love releases it. Hatred confuses life; love harmonizes it. Hatred darkens life; love illumines it."[16] Even though King fell victim to hatred, his commitment to compassion changed the world and his memory remains a constant inspiration. The same is true of Gandhi, who was assassinated in 1948. After his death, the Indian prime minister Pandit Nehru told his people:

> The light has gone out, I said, and yet I was wrong. For the light that shone in this country was no ordinary light. The light that has illumined this country for these many years will illumine this country for many more years, and a thousand years later that light will still be seen in this country, and the world will see it and it will give solace to innumerable hearts.[17]

A life that consistently refuses to succumb to the temptation of hatred has an enduring power of its own.

But what does "love" entail? Now that we have reached the twelfth step, we know that compassion cannot simply be a matter of sentiment or emotional tenderness. When Jesus tells us to love our enemies, he is commenting on the commandment in Leviticus "You must love your neighbor as yourself."[18] Leviticus is a legal text, and any talk of emotion would be as out of place as it would be in a Supreme Court ruling. In the ancient Middle East, "love" was a legal term used in international treaties: when two kings promised to "love" each other, they pledged to be helpful and loyal and to give each other practical assistance and support, even if it went against their short-term interest.

This should be within the capacity of even the most pragmatic government. In our global village, everybody is our neighbor, and it is essential to make allies of our enemies. We need to create a world democracy in which everybody's voice is heard and everybody's aspirations are taken seriously. In the last resort, this kind of "love" and "concern for everybody" will serve our best interest better than shortsighted and self-serving policies.

So during this step, we add one final stage to the meditation on the Immeasurables. After you have directed your friendship, compassion, sympathetic joy, and *upeksha* to yourself, to a person who is neutral to you, and to somebody you dislike, bring to mind an "Enemy" with a capital *E*, something or someone that seems to threaten your survival and everything you stand for. It may be a state with whom your country is at war or an oppressive imperialism; it could be a religious tradition, or a nation that has injured and terrorized your people, deprived you of basic rights, and seems bent on your destruction. We begin, as always, with ourselves. You may, with good reason, feel deep anger toward the enemy. This is the starting point from which you have to work, so acknowledge your hatred. Take note of your profound reluctance to turn this enemy into a friend. Remember that we can become twinned with an enemy and come to resemble him. Our hatred may become an alter ego, a part of our identity. Reflect on the importance of distinguishing individuals from the leaders who preach hatred, and remember that people do not choose to be born into the situation that seems so inimical to you; it is one of the givens of life. Each member of an enemy nation, each adherent of every religious tradition, has his or her own personal history of distress and may be suffering from the situation as much as you. Does your enemy have a history of oppression, exploitation, exile, or persecution? Has your nation contributed to this? Finally, consider the flaws of your own people: Is your hatred another instance of the splinter and the plank? We are aiming at *upeksha,* an impartial, fair-minded assessment of the situation in the cause of peace. Try to wish for your enemy's well-being and happiness; try to develop a sense of responsibility for your enemy's pain.

This is the supreme test of compassion. At first it may seem impossible. But if you have the will and determination to overcome your own hatred, this exercise can over time change your patterns of hostility, suspicion, and disgust. As we saw in the story of Yaakov and Esau, our enemy is our other self. We are bound together by our enmity and share the same predicament.

During the Vietnam War, Thich Nhat Hanh, a Vietnamese Buddhist monk, performed the meditation on the Immeasurables for the soldiers of his country—but he contemplated the plight of the American troops too, and made himself desire their safety and well-being. Once you realize that your enemy is also suffering, you look into his eyes and see a mirror image of your own distress. In this way, you realize that he too deserves compassion. Eventually it became clear to Thich Nhat Hanh that only one course of action was possible: to work to end the war.[19] Today some of the Israelis and Palestinians who have lost children in the conflict have come together, their suffering creating a bond that transcends political divisions, in order to work for peace. On the Indian subcontinent, Indians and Pakistanis, shocked by the terrorism they have both experienced, are campaigning together for peace between their countries.

It is now time to investigate your enemy, using the "science of compassion" in the same way as you began to get to know your "adopted" foreign nation or tradition during the tenth step. Start with the realization of how little you really know and find out more about the history of your enemy. Again, you may discover that matters are more complex than you supposed. At each point, keep asking "But why?" until you have built up an understanding of the context that gives you an empathetic grasp of your enemy's situation. We can never condone cruelty, ruthless violence, terrorism, or systemic injustice, but remember that you, your own nation, and your own tradition also have flaws and, in all likelihood, have committed serious crimes against others in the past or, perhaps, even in the present. Is there great suffering in your enemy's history? Remember that in a threatening environment, the human brain becomes permanently organized for aggression. Has this happened to your enemy? Remember also the importance of visiting the "shadow" in your own mind. Perhaps, in different circumstances, you too would be capable of evil actions.

Retaliation is likely only to exacerbate the hatred and violence activated by the threat mechanism. On September 11, 2001, for example, there were demonstrations and expressions of sympathy for the United States in countries all over the world, including Palestine and Iran. If there had been a nonviolent and openhanded response to the attacks on the Twin Towers instead of a military offensive, might the outcome have been different? Remember Confucius's words: if you seek to establish yourself, then seek to establish others. Humiliating the enemy can be dangerous. The harsh conditions inflicted on Germany by the Treaty of Versailles after the First World War gave birth to the conditions that helped to bring Adolf Hitler to power. We need to find a way to ensure that all peoples enjoy the treatment that we wish for ourselves.

There is much talk of the need for dialogue as a way of improving international relations. But will it be Socratic or an aggressive dialogue that seeks to humiliate, manipulate, or defeat? Are we prepared to "make place for the other," or are we determined simply to impose our own will? An essential part of this dialogue must be the effort to *listen*. We have to make a more serious effort to hear one another's narratives. All too often, when the enemy starts to tell his story, the other side interrupts, shouts him down, objects, and denounces it as false and inaccurate. But like any mythos, a story often reflects the inner meaning of an event rather than factual, historical accuracy. As any psychoanalyst knows, stories of pain, betrayal, and atrocity give expression to the emotional dimension of an episode, which is just as important to the speaker as what actually happened. We need to listen to the undercurrent of pain in our enemy's story. And we should be aware as well that our version of the same event is also likely to be a reflection upon our own situation and suffering rather than a dispassionate and wholly factual account.

We have to try to look carefully and deeply into our own hearts and thus learn to see the sorrow of our enemy. The Greeks were a warlike people, but they understood this. The first of their great tragic dramas to survive was Aeschylus's *The Persians*, which was presented on the festival of Dionysus in 472 BCE, just eight years after Athens had defeated the Persian army in the landmark battle of Salamis. But before the Athenian victory, the Persians had rampaged through Athens, pillaging, burning, and trashing the city and obliterating all the beautiful new temples on the Acropolis. Yet in his drama, Aeschylus asks the audience to weep for the Persians and asks them to see Salamis from the enemy's point of view. Xerxes, the defeated Persian general, his mother, Atossa, and the ghost of the late Persian king Darius are all treated with sympathy and respect. All speak of the piercing sorrow of bereavement, which has stripped away the veneer of security to reveal the terror that lies at the heart of human life. In the spirit of the *Daodejing*, there is no triumphalism and no gloating. The Persians are presented as a people in mourning. Greece and Persia are described as "sisters of one race . . . flawless in beauty and grace."[20]

But Aeschylus hints that Greece and Persia are also bound together by a shared lust for power. Darius warns against the dangers of *hubris* ("overweening pride"), admitting that when he invaded Greece he brought disaster on his people by failing to observe the divinely sanctioned boundaries of his empire.

. . . Let no man,
Scorning the fortune that he has, in greed for more
Pour out his wealth in utter waste. Zeus throned on high
Sternly chastises arrogant, boastful men.[21]

But Athens was equally guilty of pride and greed. Some Athenians were beginning to feel uneasy about their violation of the Delian League, which had originally been designed to bring the Greek city-states together against the Persian threat and to foster friendship and brotherhood between them. But after Salamis, Athens had started to invade other poleis and was using the spoils of battle to fund its expensive building projects.[22] Aeschylus had made it clear to the audience that his city was in no position to pontificate self-righteously over the sins of the enemy.

We need this spirit today. Centuries before Aeschylus, Homer had shown what could happen when you reached out to the enemy in time of war. The *Iliad*, his eighth-century epic, tells the story of a small incident in the ten-year war between the Greeks and the Trojans. Achilles, the chief warrior on the Greek side, quarrels with King Agamemnon and, in a fit of egotistic pique, withdraws his men from the army and sulks in his tent. This had disastrous consequences for the Greeks, and in the ensuing confusion, Achilles' beloved friend Patroclus is killed by Hector, one of the Trojan princes. Achilles becomes almost mad with guilt, grief, and rage. He challenges Hector to a duel, kills him, and horribly mutilates his corpse by dragging it round and round Patroclus's grave in full view of the Trojan royal family, who are watching from the city walls. He then refuses to give the body back to the family for burial, which means that Hector's spirit will never know rest.

But one night, King Priam of Troy enters the Greek camp incognito and makes his way to Achilles' tent to beg for the body of his son. To the astonishment of Achilles' companions, the old man throws off his disguise and falls at the feet of his son's slayer, weeping and kissing the hands that "were dangerous and man-slaughtering and had killed so many of his sons."[23] His utter abasement awakens in Achilles a profound grief for his own dead father, and he begins to weep too, "now for his own father, now again for Patroclus."[24] The two men cling together, mourning their dead. Then Achilles rises, takes Priam's hand, and raises him gently to his feet "in pity for the grey head and the grey beard."[25] Carefully, tenderly, he hands over Hector's body, concerned that its weight might be too much for the frail old man. And then the two enemies look at each other in silent awe:

> *Priam, son of Dardanos, gazed upon Achilles, wondering*
> *At his size and beauty, for he seemed like an outright*
>   *vision*
> *Of gods. Achilles in turn gazed on Dardanian Priam*
> *And wondered, as he saw his brave looks, and listened to*
>   *him talking.*[26]

In the midst of a deadly war, the shared suffering and pity of it all had enabled each man to transcend his hatred and see the sacred mystery of his enemy.

A Last Word

The Trojan War did not end with the embrace of Achilles and Priam. The fighting continued the next day and would not cease until the beautiful city of Troy was destroyed. We have moments of insight that take us beyond our self-absorption, but it is all too easy to fall back into our old ways. Yaakov's epiphany at Peniel was the high point of his life, but he was unable to build upon it. The authors of Genesis show that his later life was characterized by a debilitating egotism. When his daughter Dinah is raped, Yaakov is more concerned about his standing in the region than with her suffering. Instead of treating all members of his family with equal affection, he shows a self-indulgent partiality to his favorite son that has almost fatal consequences.

This does not mean that we end on a depressing note. It

is rather a reminder that the attempt to become a compassionate human being is a lifelong project. It is not achieved in an hour or a day—or even in twelve steps. It is a struggle that will last until our dying hour. Nearly every day we will fail, but we cannot give up like Yaakov; we must pick ourselves up and start again. If you have followed the steps carefully, you have come a long way. But the process is not over. You will have to work at all twelve steps continuously for the rest of your life—learning more about compassion, surveying your world anew, struggling with self-hatred and discouragement. Never mind loving your enemies—sometimes loving your nearest and dearest selflessly and patiently will be a struggle!

I hope I have shown in this book that compassion *is* possible, and that even in our torn and conflicted world some people have achieved heroic levels of empathy, forgiveness, and "concern for everybody." We are not doomed to live in misery, hatred, greed, and envy. As Xunzi insisted, any one of us can become a sage, an avatar of compassion. When we feel cast down by our pain and by the misery that we see all around us, we should experience our dejection as a call to further effort. The mythos of compassion tells us what to do. Instead of becoming depressed by our repeated failures, we should remember that constant practice does indeed make perfect and that if we persevere, we too can become a force for good in the world.

King Pasenadi, the Buddha's friend, fell into a deep depression when his wife died. He no longer felt at home anywhere and had taken to leaving his palace and driving for miles with his army, going aimlessly from one place to another. One day, he was driving through a park filled with huge tropical trees. Dismounting from his carriage, the king walked among their great roots, which were themselves as tall as a man, and felt consoled. These ancient trees "inspired trust and confidence." "They were quiet; no discordant voices disturbed their peace; they gave out a sense of being apart from the ordinary world, a place where one could take refuge" from the cruelties of life. As he contemplated these marvelous old trees, the king was reminded of the Buddha: his inner quiet had raised him above petty disturbances in a world of clamorous egotism, and you could shelter with him in a crisis.[1]

A person who is impartial, fair, calm, gentle, serene, accepting, and openhearted is indeed a refuge. In the person of the Buddha, who had gone beyond the limitations and partialities of selfhood, many experienced a humanity that made them feel that life was endurable. A truly compassionate person touches a chord in us that resonates with some of our deepest yearnings. People flock to such individuals, because they seem to offer a haven of peace in a violent, angry world. This is the ideal to which we aspire, and it is not beyond our capacity. But even if we achieve only a fraction of this enlightenment and leave the world marginally better because we have lived in it, our lives will have been worthwhile. There is no more to be said. We know what we have to do. This is the end of the book, but our work is just beginning.

ACKNOWLEDGMENTS

As always, a full-hearted thanks to my agents, Felicity
Bryan, Peter Ginsberg, and Andrew Nurnberg, and my edi-
tors, Jane Garrett, Will Sulkin, and Robbert Ammerlaan,
who have supported me so devotedly over the years. I am
also most grateful to all the people who have worked on
this book with such professional expertise: At the Bodley
Head, special thanks to Jörg Hensgen for his painstak-
ing, thorough, and imaginative work on the manuscript,
Kay Peddle (assistant editor), Beth Humphries (copy editor), and Anna Crone (jacket designer); and at Knopf, El-
len Feldman (production editor), Maggie Hinders (text
designer), Barbara de Wilde (jacket designer), Louise Col-
lazo (copy editor), and Claire Bradley Ong (production
manager), who worked to the standard of excellence that
I have come to expect from Knopf but hope I shall never
take for granted. Thanks too to Michele Topham, Carole
Robinson, and Jackie Head in Felicity Bryan's office, and
to Leslie Levine, Jane Garrett's assistant, for their kindness and endless patience. Thanks in advance also to the

publicists: Chloe Johnson Hill, Kim Thornton, Sheila Kay, and Francien Schuursma, who I know will work with their usual skill and commitment when the book is published.

But I must also thank all those who have worked with me on the Charter for Compassion. First, my sincere gratitude to everybody at TED, who from the very beginning saw potential in what some would have regarded as a quixotic project, especially Chris Anderson, Amy Novogratz (to whom this book is dedicated), Casson Rosenblatt, and Daniel Mitchell. Your generosity, commitment, and creativity never cease to astonish me. It has also been a great joy to work with everybody at the Fetzer Institute, with special thanks to Susan Trabucchi (former senior program officer) for her invaluable commitment and practical insight during my first months with Fetzer, Gillian Gonda (program officer), and Amy Ferguson (communications specialist). Thanks too to Simon Cohen and Lance McPherson at Global Tolerance for their superb input; and to Emily Hawkins at Sunshine, Sachs & Associates. Finally, thanks to James Berrill for achieving the near-impossible feat of collating the myriad contributions made to the draft charter by the general public in preparation for the meeting of the Council of Conscience in Vevey, Switzerland.

It is unfortunately impossible to thank all the people in over 150 partner organizations and the individual ambassadors who are working so tirelessly to incorporate the message of the charter into their own programs. We are immensely grateful for the support and endorsement of H. H. the Dalai Lama and the Dalai Lama Foundation. I must give special thanks to Badr Jafar, CEO of Crescent

Petroleum, for his extraordinary commitment and pragmatic genius in promoting the charter in the Middle East; Amin Hashwani for his relentless and innovative work for peace in Pakistan; Ambassador Mussie Hailu of Ethiopia, who declared April 5 Golden Rule Day in the United Nations and has energetically promoted the charter in Africa; Danielle Lauren of Sydney, Australia; Janet Allinson in Canada; all my new friends at the Compassionate Action Network in Seattle for their outstanding leadership; the United Religious Initiative; Mozes & Aäronkerk in Amsterdam; and my friends at the Chautauqua Institution for their impressive work and ongoing counsel. It is a joy and privilege to work with each and every one of you.

Finally, I am most grateful to the members of the Council of Conscience, who composed the charter. First, my dear friend the Reverend Dr. Joan Brown Campbell, Director of the Department of Religion at the Chautauqua Institution, who committed herself heart and soul to the charter from day one and chaired the Vevey meeting with such brilliance and acumen. The very first person I approached about the charter was Archbishop Emeritus Desmond Tutu, whose immediate and generous response gave the charter a credibility at an early stage that it might not otherwise have had. And my most sincere thanks to all the Councillors whose wisdom and insight were an inspiration: Salman Ahmed, musician and social activist; Ali Asani, Professor of the Practice of Indo-Muslim Languages and Culture at Harvard University; Sadhvi Chaitanya, Spiritual Director of Arsha Vijan Mandiram; the Right Reverend John Bryson Chane, Episcopal Bishop of Washington, D.C.; Sister Joan

Chittister, Founder and Director of Benetvision; His Excellency Sheikh Ali Gomaa, Grand Mufti of the Arab Republic of Egypt; Mohsen Kadivar, Professor of Religious Studies at Duke University; Chandra Muzaffar, President of the International Movement for a Just World; Baroness Julia Neuberger, Prime Minister's Champion for Volunteering, U.K.; Tariq Ramadan, Professor of Contemporary Islamic Studies at Oxford University; Rabbi David Saperstein, Director of the Religious Action Center of Reform Judaism in Washington, D.C.; Rabbi Awraham Soetendorp, Rabbi of the Reform Jewish Community of The Hague; Reverend Peter Storey, former President of the Methodist Church of South Africa and the South African Council of Churches; Tho Ha Vinh, Head of Training, Learning, and Development in the International Committee of the Red Cross; Tu Wei Ming, Professor of Chinese History and Philosophy and of Confucian Studies at Harvard University; and Jean Zaru, presiding Clerk of the Ramallah Friends Meeting. I shall never forget our conversation at Vevey, which was a model of Socratic and compassionate discourse. I look forward to working with you all in the future.

And last—but for me far from least—thanks to everybody at My Ideal Dog: Eve, Gary, Stacey, and Amy Mott and Michelle Stevenson, who make it possible for me to promote the charter by giving Poppy such a wonderful second home and have taught me so much about compassion for animals.

NOTES

PREFACE *Wish for a Better World*

1. Information about the activities of the charter can be found on
   www.charterforcompassion.org.
2. Confucius, Analects 15.23. Unless otherwise stated, all quotations
   from the Analects are taken from Arthur Waley, trans. and ed., *The
   Analects of Confucius* (New York, 1992).
3. Analects 4.15, as translated by A. C. Graham, *Disputers of the Tao:
   Philosophical Argument in Ancient China* (La Salle, Ill., 1989), p. 21.
4. Tu Wei-Ming, *Confucian Thought: Selfhood as Creative Transformation* (Albany, 1985), p. 84.
5. Analects 12.3.
6. The Buddha's dates are now disputed. Western scholars used to
   think that he was born in about 563 BCE, but recent scholarship
   indicates that he could have lived a century later. Heinz Berchant,
   "The Date of the Buddha Reconsidered," *Indologia Taurinensen* 10
   (n.d.).
7. Richard Dawkins, *The God Delusion* (London and New York, 2006),
   p. 221.
8. E. O. Wilson, *On Human Nature* (Cambridge, Mass., 1978), p. 156.
9. Paul Gilbert, *The Compassionate Mind: A New Approach to Life's
   Challenges* (London, 2009).
10. August Comte, *A General View of Positivism,* trans. J. H. Bridges
    (London, 1865), p. 16.

11. Mircea Eliade, *A History of Religious Ideas*, 3 vols., trans. Willard R. Trask (Chicago and London, 1978, 1982, 1985), 1:7–8, 24; Joseph Campbell, *Historical Atlas of World Mythologies*, 2 vols. (New York, 1988), 1:48–49; Joseph Campbell, with Bill Moyers, *The Power of Myth* (New York, 1988), pp. 72–70, 85–87.

12. Barbara L. Frederickson, "The Broaden and Build Theory of Positive Emotions," *Philosophical Transactions of the Royal Society of London* 359 (2004); Alan M. Isen, Andrew S. Rosensweig, and Mark J. Young, "The Influence of Positive Affect on Clinical Problem Solving," *Medical Decision Making* 11 (1991); George E. Vaillant, M.D., *Spiritual Evolution: A Scientific Defense of Faith* (New York, 2008), pp. 3–46.

13. P. Broca, "Anatomie comparée des circonvolutions cérébrales: Le grand lobe limbique," *Revue Anthropologique* 1 (1878).

14. Recent research indicates that the limbic system is not as clearly located and defined as Broca and MacLean imagined.

15. Antonio Damasio, *Descartes' Error* (New York, 1994); Eric R. Kandel, James H. Schwartz, and Thomas M. Jessell, *Principles of Neural Science* (New York, 2000).

16. Gilbert, *Compassionate Mind*, pp. 42–44.

17. Vaillant, *Spiritual Evolution*, pp. 42–46, 94–95; Elliot Sober and David S. Wilson, *Unto Others: The Evolution and Psychology of Unselfish Behavior* (Cambridge, Mass., 1998).

18. Gilbert, *Compassionate Mind*, pp. 170–71; D. C. Bell, "Evolution of Care-giving Behavior," *Personality and Social Psychology Review* 5 (2001).

19. Gilbert, *Compassionate Mind*, pp. 168–71.

20. R. A. Depue and J. V. Morrone-Strupinsky, "A Neurobehavioural Model of Affiliative Bonding," *Behavioral and Brain Sciences* 28 (2005); M. Kosfield, M. Heinrichs, P. J. Zak, U. Frisbacher, and E. Fehr, "Oxytocin Increases Trust in Humans," *Nature Neuroscience* 435 (June 2005).

21. L. Cozolino, *The Neuroscience of Human Relationships: Attachment and the Developing Brain* (New York, 2007); S. Gerhart, *Why Love Matters: How Affection Shapes a Baby's Brain* (London, 2004).

22. Tania Singer, "Empathy for Pain Involves the Affective but Not Sensory Components of Pain," *Science* 303 (2004); James T. Kaplan and Marco Iacoboni, "Getting a Grip on the Other Minds: Mirror

Neurons, Intention Understanding, and Cognitive Empathy," *Social Neuroscience* 1 (2006).

23. *The Book of Mencius* 2A 6, in D. C. Lau, trans., *Mencius* (London, 1970).

24. H. H. the Dalai Lama, *Ethics for the New Millennium* (New York, 1999), p. 19.

THE FIRST STEP *Learn About Compassion*

1. For an extended explanation of mythology, see Johannes Sloek, *Devotional Language,* trans. Henrik Mossin (Berlin and New York, 1996), pp. 53–96; Joseph Campbell, with Bill Moyers, *The Power of Myth* (New York, 1988); and my own *A Short History of Myth* (London and New York, 1995).

2. Mircea Eliade, *Myths, Dreams, and Mysteries: The Encounter Between Contemporary Faiths and Archaic Realities,* trans. Philip Mairet (London, 1960), p. 225.

3. I have explored this more fully in *The Great Transformation: The Beginning of Our Religious Traditions* (London and New York, 2006).

4. Paul Gilbert, *The Compassionate Mind: A New Approach to Life's Challenges* (London, 2009), pp. 45–46.

5. Karl Jaspers, *The Origin and Goal of History,* trans. Michael Bullock (London, 1953), pp. 1–70.

6. J. C. Heesterman, "Ritual, Revelation, and the Axial Age," in S. N. Eisenstadt, ed., *The Origins and Diversity of Axial Age Civilizations* (Albany, 1986), p. 403.

7. Patrick Olivelle, ed. and trans., *Upanishads* (Oxford and New York, 1996), p. xxix. All quotations from the Upanishads are taken from this translation.

8. Ibid.; Michael Witzel, "Vedas and Upanishads," in Gavin Flood, ed., *The Blackwell Companion to Hinduism* (Oxford, 2003), pp. 85–86.

9. Brhadaranyaka Upanishad (BU) 3.4.

10. Jan Gonda, *Change and Continuity in Indian Religion* (The Hague, 1965), p. 200; Louis Renou, "Sur la notion de *brahman,*" *Journal Asiatique* 237 (1940).

11. BU 4.4.23–35.

12. Ibid.

13. BU 4.4.5–7.

14. Chandogya Upanishad (CU) 8.7.1–8.11.3.

15. CU 8.15; J. C. Heesterman, *The Broken World of Sacrifice: An Essay in Ancient Indian Ritual* (Chicago and London, 1993), p. 170.

16. Mircea Eliade, *Yoga: Immortality and Freedom,* trans. Willard R. Trask (London, 1958); Edward Conze, *Buddhist Meditation* (London, 1956).

17. Yoga Sutra 2.42 in Eliade, *Yoga,* p. 52.

18. Majjhima Nikaya (MN) 36. The Pali scriptures include four collections of the Buddha's sermons (Majjhima Nikaya, Digha Nikaya, Anguttara Nikaya [AN], and Samutta Nikaya) and an anthology of minor works. The quotations from the Pali Canon are my own version of the texts cited.

19. Joseph Campbell, *Oriental Mythology: The Masks of God* (New York, 1962), p. 236.

20. AN 9.3; MN 38.41.

21. AN 8.7.3.

22. Robert Emmons, *Thanks! How the New Science of Gratitude Can Make You Happier* (Boston, 2007), p. 4; George E. Vaillant, *Spiritual Evolution: A Scientific Defense of Faith* (New York, 2008), pp. 5–6.

23. Astasahasrika 15.293, in Edward Conze, *Buddhism: Its Essence and Development* (Oxford, 1951), p. 125.

24. Jacques Gernet, *Ancient China: From the Beginnings to the Empire,* trans. Raymond Rudorff (London, 1968), pp. 71–75.

25. Marcel Granet, *Chinese Civilization,* trans. Kathleen E. Innes and Mabel R. Brailsford (London and New York, 1951), pp. 261–79.

26. Remarks of Jacques Gernet, reported in Jean-Pierre Vernant, *Myth and Society in Ancient Greece,* 3rd ed., trans. Janet Lloyd (New York, 1996), pp. 80–82.

27. Confucius, Analects 12.1. Translation suggested by Benjamin I. Schwartz, *The World of Thought in Ancient China* (Cambridge, Mass., and London, 1985), p. 77.

28. Analects 12.2.

29. Analects 6.28.

30. Tu Wei-Ming, *Confucian Thought: Selfhood as Creative Transformation* (Albany, 1985), pp. 115–16.

31. Ibid., pp. 57–58; Huston Smith, *The World's Religions: Our Great Wisdom Traditions* (San Francisco, 1991), pp. 180–81.

32. Analects 6.20; 16.12.
33. Analects 7.29.
34. Analects 8.7.
35. Analects 9.10.
36. Jacques Gernet, *A History of Chinese Civilization*, trans. J. R. Foster and Charles Hartman, 2nd ed. (Cambridge, U.K., and New York, 1996), pp. 62–67; Gernet, *Ancient China*, pp. 93–94, 96–101.
37. *The Book of Mozi* 3.16, trans. Fung Yu Lan, in *A Short History of Chinese Philosophy*, ed. and trans. Derk Bodde (New York, 1976), p. 55.
38. A. C. Graham, *Disputers of the Tao: Philosophical Argument in Ancient China* (La Salle, Ill., 1989), p. 41.
39. *Mozi* 15.1–15, in Burton Watson, trans. and ed., *Mo-Tzu: Basic Writings* (New York, 1963).
40. *Mozi* 16, Watson translation.
41. *The Book of Xunzi* 15.72, in Burton Watson, ed. and trans., *Xunzi: Basic Writings* (New York, 2003).
42. *Xunzi* 23:1–4.
43. Ibid.
44. *Xunzi* 17.44.
45. *Xunzi* 21:28–30.
46. *Xunzi* 19.63.
47. *Xunzi* 19.17–79.
48. B. Shabbat 31a, in A. Cohen, ed., *Everyman's Talmud* (New York, 1975).
49. Sifra on Leviticus 19:11.
50. Genesis 5:1 *Genesis Rabbah*, Berishit 24.7.
51. Aboth de Rabbi Nathan I. N, 11a, in C. G. Montefiore and H. Loewe, eds., *A Rabbinic Anthology* (New York, 1976).
52. Hosea 6:6.
53. M. Sotah 8.7; M. Sanhedrin 1.5; B. Sanhedrin.
54. Louis Jacobs, "Peace," in *Jewish Values* (London, 1960), pp. 155–60.
55. Sifra on Leviticus 19:17.
56. Aboth de Rabbi Nathan 2.16.
57. Ibid., 23; Cohen translation.
58. Mekhilta on Exodus 20:13.
59. B. Sanhedrin 4.5.
60. M. Baba Metziah 58b; M. Arkhim 15b.
61. Matthew 7:12; Luke 6:31.

62. Matthew 22:34–40; Mark 12:29–31; Luke 10:25–28.
63. Matthew 7:1.
64. Matthew 25:31–46.
65. Matthew 19:16–22; Mark 10:13–16; Luke 18:18–23.
66. Matthew 5:39–40. All quotations from the Bible are taken from *The Jerusalem Bible* (London, 1966).
67. Matthew 5:43–48. Note: the written Torah does *not* condone the hating of enemies. "Hate your enemy" was probably an Aramaic idiom meaning "you need not love your enemies."
68. Philippians 2:6–11.
69. Philippians 2:2–4.
70. I Corinthians 13:1–3.
71. Acts 4.32.
72. Acts 2.44–45.
73. Augustine, *On Christian Doctrine*, trans. D. W. Robertson (Indianapolis, 1958), p. 30.
74. Toshiko Izutsu, *Ethico-Religious Concepts in the Qur'an* (Montreal and Kingston, Ont., 2002), p. 46.
75. Ibid., pp. 28–45.
76. Ibid., pp. 28, 68–69.
77. Qur'an 14:47; 39:37; 15:79; 30:47; 44:16.
78. Qur'an 90:13–17.
79. Qur'an 25:63, in Muhammad Asad, trans., *The Message of the Qur'an* (Gibraltar, 1980).
80. Qur'an 55:10.
81. Qur'an 22:39–40.
82. Qur'an 16:125–26.
83. Qur'an 48:26; Asad translation.
84. Qur'an 20:114; cf. 75:17–19.

THE SECOND STEP *Look at Your Own World*

1. Joseph Campbell, *The Hero with a Thousand Faces* (Princeton, N.J., 1949).
2. Majjhima Nikaya 26, 36, 85, 100.
3. Matthew 5:1–10.

4. Confucius, Analects 2.7.
5. Analects 2.8.

THE THIRD STEP *Compassion for Yourself*

1. Leviticus 19:18.
2. Sheila MacLeod, *The Art of Starvation* (London, 1981).
3. Quoted by Youssef M. Choueri, *Islamic Fundamentalism* (London, 1990), p. 36.
4. *Vinaya:* Mahavagga 1.6 (this book is part of the *Vinaya Pitaka, The Book of Monastic Discipline,* which codifies the rules of the Buddhist order); Samyutta Nikaya 22.59.
5. Norman Cohn, *The Pursuit of the Millennium: Revolutionary Millenarians and Mystical Anarchists of the Middle Ages* (London, 1970), pp. 76–78, 80, 86–87.
6. M. Montgomery Watt, *The Influence of Islam on Medieval Europe* (Edinburgh, 1972), pp. 74–86.
7. *Vinaya:* Mahavagga 1.6.
8. Madhyama Agama 86, in Thich Nhat Hanh, *Teachings on Love* (Berkeley, 2007), p. 13.
9. H. H. the Dalai Lama, *Ethics for the New Millennium* (New York, 1999), p. 24.
10. Ibid.
11. Ibid., p. 26.
12. I Corinthians 13:4–7.
13. Majjhima Nikaya 1.
14. *Vinaya:* Mahavagga 1.6.
15. M. Avoth 6.1, trans. Michael Fishbane, "From Scribalism to Rabbinism," in *The Garments of Torah: Essays in Biblical Hermeneutics* (Bloomington and Indianapolis, 1989).
16. I Philippians 2:6–11.
17. Cyril of Jerusalem, *Mystagogical Catechesis* 3.1.
18. Maximus the Confessor, *Ambigua* 42.
19. *The Book of Xunzi* 21:34–39, in Burton Watson, trans. and ed., *Xunzi: Basic Writings* (New York, 2003).
20. Anguttara Nikaya 4.36.

THE FOURTH STEP *Empathy*

1. *Agamemnon* 177–84, in Robert Fagles, trans., *Aeschylus: The Oresteia* (London, 1975).
2. Charles Segal, "Catharsis, Audience and Closure in Greek Tragedy," in M. S. Silk, ed., *Tragedy and the Tragic: Greek Theatre and Beyond* (Oxford, 1996), pp. 157–58; Oliver Taplin, "Comedy and the Tragic," in Silk, *Tragedy,* pp. 198–99.
3. Euripides, *Medea* 1021–80; Bernard Seidensticker, "Peripeteia and Tragic Dialectic in Euripidean Tragedy," in Silk, *Tragedy,* pp. 387–88.
4. Aristotle, *Rhetoric* 1385b.11–1386b.7.
5. Euripides, *Heracles* 1233–38, 1398–1428, in Philip Vellacott, trans., *Euripides: Medea and Other Plays* (London and New York, 1963).
6. Segal, "Catharsis," pp. 166–68; Claude Calame, "Vision, Blindness and Mask: The Radicalisation of the Emotions," in Silk, *Tragedy,* pp. 19–31; Richard Buxton, "What Can You Rely on in *Oedipus Rex*?" in Silk, *Tragedy,* pp. 38–49.
7. Sophocles, *King Oedipus* 1297, 1312, 1299, 1321, in E. F. Watling, trans., *Sophocles: The Theban Plays* (London, 1947).
8. Jean-Pierre Vernant, with Pierre Vidal-Naquet, *Myth and Tragedy in Ancient Greece,* trans. Janet Lloyd (New York, 1990), pp. 113–17.
9. H. H. the Dalai Lama, *Ethics for the New Millennium* (New York, 1999), p. 64.
10. Albert Schweitzer, *Reverence for Life* (New York, 1965), p. 1.
11. Albert Schweitzer, *Out of My Life and Thought* (New York, 1953), p. 70.
12. Qur'an 93:5–20, in Michael Sells, ed. and trans., *Approaching the Qur'an: The Early Revelations* (Ashland, Ore., 1999).
13. Patty Anglin, with Joe Musser, *Acres of Hope: The Miraculous Story of One Family's Gift of Love to Children Without Hope* (Uhrichsville, Ohio, 1999), p. 29.

THE SIXTH STEP *Action*

1. Wordsworth, *The Prelude,* book XII, "Imagination and Taste, How Impaired and Restored," lines 207–15, in Thomas Hutchinson, ed.,

Wordsworth: Poetical Works, revised by Ernest De Selincourt (Oxford, 1966).

2. Wordsworth, "Lines Composed a Few Miles Above Tintern Abbey, on Revisiting the Banks of the Wye During a Tour," lines 32–34, ibid.

THE SEVENTH STEP *How Little We Know*

1. Marshall G. S. Hodgson, *The Venture of Islam: Conscience and History in a World Civilization,* 3 vols. (Chicago and London, 1974), 1:379. The phrase "science of compassion" is taken from Louis Massignon, "Les Nusayris," in Claude Cahen, ed., *L'Elaboration de l'Islam* (Paris, 1961).
2. I have discussed this in detail in the final chapter of *The Spiral Staircase* (London and New York, 2004).
3. Plato, *Apology* 21a, trans. G. M. A. Grube, in John M. Cooper, ed., *Plato: Complete Works* (Indianapolis, 1997).
4. Plato, Seventh Letter 344, in Walter Hamilton, trans., *Plato: Phaedrus and Letters VII and VIII* (London, 1973).
5. Ibid., 341.
6. Ibid., 29d, 30e–31c, 36c.
7. Ibid., 38a.
8. *The Book of Zhuangzi* 6.93, in David Hinton, trans., *Chuang-Tsu: The Inner Chapters* (Washington, D.C., 1998).
9. Ibid., 17.3.
10. Ibid., 2.1–3.
11. *The Book of Zhuangzi* 6.80, in Martin Palmer, with Elizabeth Brenilly, trans., *The Book of Chuang Tzu* (London and New York, 1996).
12. Ibid., 1.21.
13. Ibid., 7.32; 13.2–6; 33.56.
14. Quoted in Huston Smith, *Beyond the Post-Modern Mind* (Wheaton, Ill., 1989), p. 8.
15. Paul Davies in an interview with Bel Mooney, ed., *Devout Sceptics* (London, 2003), p. 57.
16. Brian Magee, *Confessions of a Philosopher: A Journey Through Western Philosophy* (London, 1997), p. 561.

17. Karl R. Popper, *Unended Quest: An Intellectual Autobiography* (London, 1992), p. 145.

18. Albert Einstein, "Strange Is Our Situation Here on Earth," in Jaroslav Pelikan, ed., *Modern Religious Thought* (Boston, 1990), p. 225.

19. Ibid.

20. Albert Schweitzer, *Out of My Life and Thought* (New York, 1953), p. 170.

21. William Shakespeare, *Hamlet, Prince of Denmark,* act 2, scene 2, lines 304–9, in Peter Alexander, ed., *William Shakespeare: The Complete Works* (London and Glasgow, 1951).

22. Ibid.

23. Ibid., act 3, scene 2, lines 341–63.

24. Iris Murdoch, *The Bell,* with an introduction by A. S. Byatt (London, 1999), p. 196.

THE EIGHTH STEP *How Should We Speak to One Another?*

1. Pierre Hadot, *Philosophy as a Way of Life: Spiritual Exercises from Socrates to Foucault,* intro. and ed. Arnold I. Davidson, trans. Michael Chase (Oxford, 1995), pp. 91–93.

2. Plato, *Meno* 75c–d, in "Meno," trans. G. M. Grube, in John M. Cooper, ed., *Plato: Complete Works* (Indianapolis, 1997).

3. Plato, Seventh Letter 344, in Walter Hamilton, trans., *Plato: Phaedrus and Letters VII and VIII* (London, 1973).

4. Tu Wei Ming, *Confucian Thought: Selfhood as Creative Transformation* (Albany, 1985), p. 84.

5. Confucius, Analects 7.33.

6. Majjhima Nikaya 89.

7. Samyutta Nikaya 3.1–8.

8. Anguttara Nikaya 3.65.

9. I have discussed this more fully in *The Battle for God: A History of Fundamentalism* (London and New York, 2000).

10. W. V. O. Quine, *Word and Object* (New York, 1960), pp. 9–12.

11. A definition of the "principle of charity" by N. L. Wilson, in Ian Hacking, *Why Does Language Matter to Philosophy?* (Cambridge, U.K., 1975), p. 148.

12. Donald Davidson, *Inquiries into Truth and Interpretation* (Oxford, 1984), p. 148.

13. Ibid., p. 197.

14. Gerald L. Bruns, "Midrash and Allegory: The Beginnings of Scriptural Interpretation," in Robert Alter and Frank Kermode, eds., *The Literary Guide to the Bible* (London, 1987), pp. 639–42.

15. I Corinthians 13:4–6.

THE NINTH STEP *Concern for Everybody*

1. Qur'an 49:13, in Muhammad Asad, trans., *The Message of the Qur'an* (Gibraltar, 1980).

2. H. H. the Dalai Lama, *An Open Heart: Practicing Compassion in Everyday Life* (New York and Boston, 2001), pp. 9–11.

3. I have discussed this more fully in *The Battle for God: A History of Fundamentalism* (New York and London, 2000), pp. 330–32.

4. Leviticus 19:18.

5. Matthew 7:2–5.

6. Confucius, Analects 6.28.

7. You can find a survey of the different versions of this story in Annemarie Schimmel, *And Muhammad Is His Messenger: The Veneration of the Prophet in Islamic Piety* (Chapel Hill, N.C., and London, 1985), pp. 155–79. See also my *Muhammad: A Prophet for Our Time* (New York and London, 2006), pp. 81–86.

8. Qur'an 17:1; 53:5–18.

9. W. Montgomery Watt, *Muhammad's Mecca: History in the Qur'an* (Edinburgh, 1988), p. 25.

10. Michael Sells, trans. and ed., *Approaching the Qur'an: The Early Revelations* (Ashland, Ore., 1999), pp. xvii–xviii.

11. *Ilahinama*, quoted in Schimmel, *Muhammad Is His Messenger*, p. 168.

12. Qur'an 2:109.

13. R. A. Nicholson, ed., *Eastern Poetry and Prose* (Cambridge, U.K., 1922), p. 148.

THE TENTH STEP *Knowledge*

1. Sutta Nipata 1.18.

THE ELEVENTH STEP *Recognition*

1. Christina Noble with Robert Coram, *Bridge Across My Sorrows: The Christina Noble Story* (London, 1994), p. 179.
2. Ibid., p. 25.
3. Ibid., p. 151.
4. Ibid., pp. 21–22.
5. Ibid., p. 307.
6. Ibid., p. 306.
7. Genesis 18:1–8.
8. Genesis 18:13, 22, 33.
9. Genesis 18:22.
10. Luke 24:13–35.
11. Genesis 32:21. For this story, I have used the translation of Everett Fox, *The Five Books of Moses* (New York, 1995), because it brings out the deeper meaning of the text more clearly than the Jerusalem Bible.
12. Genesis 32:25–32.
13. Genesis 25:23–26.
14. Genesis 25:23.
15. Genesis 33:10.

THE TWELFTH STEP *Love Your Enemies*

1. H. H. the Dalai Lama, *An Open Heart: Practicing Compassion in Everyday Life* (New York and Boston, 2001), p. 10.
2. *Daodejing* ("Classic of the Way and Its Potency") 31, in Max Kaltenmark, *Lao Tzu and Taoism,* trans. Roger Greaves (Stanford, Calif., 1969), p. 56.
3. *Daodejing* 68, ibid.
4. *Daodejing* 30, in D. C. Lau, trans., *Tao Te Ching* (London and New York, 1963).

5. *Daodejing* 1.
6. *Daodejing* 49; Lau translation.
7. *Daodejing* 13, in William Theodore de Bary and Irene Bloom, eds., *Sources of Chinese Tradition from Earliest Times to 1600* (New York, 1999), pp. 83–84.
8. Exodus 21:24.
9. Matthew 5:39.
10. Luke 6:27–31.
11. Luke 6:31, 34.
12. Louis Fischer, ed., *The Essential Gandhi* (New York, 1962), p. 193.
13. Martin Luther King Jr., *Strength to Love* (Philadelphia, 1963), pp. 40–42.
14. Ibid., p. 50.
15. Ibid., p. 52.
16. Ibid., p. 120.
17. Fischer, *Essential Gandhi,* p. 369.
18. Leviticus 19:18.
19. Thich Nhat Hanh, *Teachings on Love* (Berkeley, 2007), p. 38.
20. Aeschylus, *The Persians* 179–84, in Philip Vellacott, trans., *Aeschylus: Prometheus Bound and Other Plays* (London and New York, 1961).
21. *The Persians* 826–29.
22. Christian Meir, *Athens: A Portrait of the City in Its Golden Age,* trans. Robert and Rita Kimber (London, 1999), pp. 207–8.
23. Homer, *Iliad* 479–80, in Richard Lattimore, trans., *The Iliad of Homer* (Chicago and London, 1951).
24. *Iliad* 24.511–12.
25. *Iliad* 24.516.
26. *Iliad* 24.629–32.

A Last Word

1. Majjhima Nikaya 89.

SUGGESTIONS FOR FURTHER READING

FOR THE FIRST STEP *Learn About Compassion*

We have never learned enough about compassion. Here you may find some books to give you insight and to reinvigorate you throughout the program. Browse until you find an author whose approach you enjoy; some of these books give extensive bibliographies so that you can explore the ideas of your favorite authors in more depth and see what *they* were reading. You will probably want to start by exploring the *mythos* and teachings of your own tradition, but it can be very helpful to discover the insights of other traditions, which help you to see your own differently.

The books in this first section will give some historical background and more information about the nature of compassion.

Armstrong, Karen. *The Great Transformation: The Beginning of Our Religious Traditions*. London and New York, 2006. This is a discussion of the Axial Age that focuses on the emergence of the great themes of compassion and nonviolence.
———. *A Short History of Myth*. Edinburgh and New York, 2005.
Belkin, Samuel. *In His Image: The Jewish Philosophy of Man as Expressed in Rabbinic Tradition*. London, 1960.

Benedikt, Michael. *God Is the Good We Do: Theology of Theopraxy.* New York, 2007.

Buckman, Robert. *Can We Be Good Without God?* New York, 2002.

Campbell, Joseph, with Bill Moyers. *The Power of Myth.* New York, 1988. This is also available on video.

Eisenstadt, S. N., ed. *The Origins and Diversity of Axial Age Civilizations.* Albany, 1986.

Fingarette, Herbert. *Confucius: The Secular as Sacred.* New York, 1972.

Furnish, Victor Paul. *The Love Command in the New Testament.* Nashville and New York, 1972.

Girard, René. *Violence and the Sacred.* Trans. Patrick Gregory. Baltimore, 1977.

Holloway, Richard. *Godless Morality: Keeping Religion Out of Ethics.* Edinburgh, 1999.

Jaspers, Karl. *The Great Philosophers: The Foundations.* Ed. Hannah Arendt. Trans. Ralph Mannheim. London, 1962. This classic book consists of four quite marvelous essays on the Buddha, Confucius, Socrates, and Jesus.

———. *The Origin and Goal of History.* Trans. Michael Bullock. London, 1953. The seminal work on the Axial Age.

Nasr, Seyyed Hossein. *The Garden of Truth: The Vision and Promise of Sufism, Islam's Mystical Tradition.* San Franscisco, 2007.

Outka, Gene. *Agape: An Ethical Analysis.* New Haven, 1972.

Perkins, Pheme. *Love Commands in the New Testament.* New York, 1982.

Ramadan, Tariq. *The Quest for Meaning: Developing a Philosophy of Pluralism.* London, 2010.

Schottroff, Luise. *Essays on the Love Commandment.* Trans. Reginald H. and Ilse Fuller. Philadelphia, 1978.

Sviri, Sara. *The Taste of Hidden Things.* Inverness, Calif., 1997.

Tillich, Paul. *Love, Power and Justice.* New York and Oxford, 1963.

Tu Wei-Ming. *Confucian Thought: Selfhood as Creative Transformation.* Albany, 1985.

Vorspan, Albert, and David Saperstein. *Jewish Dimensions of Social Justice: Tough Moral Choices of Our Time.* New York, 1998.

These books focus on the practice of a compassionate way of life.

Cooper, Howard. *The Alphabet of Paradise: An A–Z of Spirituality for Everyday Life.* London, 2002.
Gandhi, Mahatma. *The Essential Gandhi.* Ed. Louis Fischer. New York, 1962.
Gyatso Tenzin, H. H. the Dalai Lama. *The Art of Happiness.* London, 1998.
———. *The Art of Happiness in a Troubled World.* New York, 2009.
———. *Ethics for the New Millennium.* New York, 1999.
———. *Healing Anger: The Power of Patience from a Buddhist Perspective.* Ithaca, N.Y., 1997.
———. *Live in a Better Way: Reflections on Truth, Love, and Happiness.* London and New York, 1999.
———. *Transforming the Mind: Teachings on Generating Compassion.* London, 2000.
King, Martin Luther, Jr. *Strength to Love.* Philadelphia, 1963.
Ladner, Lorne. *The Lost Art of Compassion: Discovering the Practice of Happiness in the Meeting of Buddhism and Psychology.* San Francisco, 2004.
Margulies, Alfred. *The Empathic Imagination.* New York, 1989.
Muhaiyaddeen, M. R. Bawa. *A Book of God's Love.* Philadelphia, 1981.
Schweitzer, Albert. *Reverence for Life.* New York, 1965.
Thich Nhat Hanh. *Anger: Wisdom for Cooling the Flames.* New York, 2001.
———. *The Art of Power.* New York, 2004.
———. *The Miracle of Mindfulness.* Boston, 1975.
———. *Peace Is Every Step: The Path of Mindfulness in Everyday Life.* New York, 1991.
———. *Taming the Tiger Within: Meditations on Transforming Difficult Emotions.* New York, 2004.
———. *Teachings on Love.* Berkeley, 2007.
———. *True Love: A Practice for Awakening the Heart.* Boston, 1997.
Tolle, Eckhart. *The Power of Now: A Guide to Spiritual Enlightenment.* London, 1999.
Tutu, Desmond M. *No Future Without Forgiveness.* New York, 1999.
———, and Mpho Tutu. *Made for Goodness: And Why This Makes a Difference.* New York, 2010.

These books look at compassion from the perspective of modern psychology and neuroscience.

Begley, Sharon. *The Plastic Mind*. London, 2009.
Browning, Don. *Religious Thought and Modern Psychologies: A Critical Conversation in the Theology of Culture*. Philadelphia, 1987.
Davidson, Richard J., and Anne Harrington, eds. *Visions of Compassion: Western Scientists and Tibetan Buddhists Examine Human Nature*. Oxford, 2002.
Gilbert, Paul. *The Compassionate Mind*. London, 2009.
Hefner, Philip. *The Human Factor: Evolution, Culture, and Religion*. Minneapolis, 1993.
Molino, Anthony, ed. *The Couch and the Tree: Dialogues in Psychoanalysis and Buddhism*. London, 1998.
Pope, Stephen. *The Evolution of Altruism and the Ordering of Love*. Washington, D.C., 1994.
Post, Stephen G. *Unlimited Love: Altruism, Compassion, and Service*. Radnor, Pa., 2003.
———, Lynn G. Underwood, Jeffrey S. Schloss, and William B. Hurlbut, eds. *Altruism and Altruistic Love: Science, Philosophy, and Religion in Dialogue*. Oxford, 2002.
Rolston, Holmes. *Genes, Genesis and God*. Cambridge, U.K., 1999.
Vaillant, George E. *Spiritual Evolution: A Scientific Defense of Faith*. New York, 2008.
Walsh, Anthony. *The Science of Love: Understanding Love and Its Effects on Mind and Body*. Buffalo, 1991.
Zornberg, Avivah Gottlieb. *The Murmuring Deep: Reflections on the Biblical Unconscious*. New York, 2009.

These books address the issues of scripture and scriptural interpretation.

Akenson, Donald Harman. *Surpassing Wonder: The Invention of the Bible and the Talmuds*. New York, San Diego, and London, 1998.
Alter, Robert, and Frank Kermode, eds. *A Literary Guide to the Bible*. London, 1987. Particularly recommended is the essay by Gerald

L. Bruns, "Midrash and Allegory: The Beginnings of Scriptural Interpretation."

Armstrong, Karen. *The Bible: A Biography.* London and New York, 2007.

Cragg, Kenneth. *The Event of the Qur'an.* Oxford, 1971. A marvelous book.

——. *Readings in the Qur'an.* London, 1988.

Fishbane, Michael. *The Exegetical Imagination: On Jewish Thought and Theology.* Cambridge, Mass., 1998.

——. *The Garments of Torah: Essays in Biblical Hermeneutics.* Bloomington and Indianapolis, 1989. Both books by Fishbane are highly recommended.

Gatje, Helmut. *The Qur'an and Its Exegesis.* Berkeley, 1976.

Holcomb, Justin S., ed. *Christian Theologies of Scripture: A Comparative Introduction.* New York and London, 2006.

Kraemer, David. *The Mind of the Talmud: An Intellectual History of the Bavli.* New York and Oxford, 1990.

Schneidewind, William M. *How the Bible Became a Book.* Cambridge, U.K., 2004.

Sells, Michael, intro. and trans. *Approaching the Qur'an: The Early Revelations.* Ashland, Ore., 1999. A superb introduction to the Qur'an, it shows how the poetry works and comes with a CD of Qur'an recitations.

Smalley, Beryl. *The Study of the Bible in the Middle Ages.* Oxford, 1941.

Smith, Wilfred Cantwell. *What Is Scripture? A Comparative Approach.* London, 1993.

Tabataba'i, Muhammad H. *Qur'an in Islam.* London, 1988.

CONCERN FOR EVERYBODY

During the tenth step, Knowledge, I recommended an exercise based on this list, but of course some readers will prefer to search out books for themselves. If you feel daunted by the list, I have marked with an asterisk those books that I think will be a good introduction and starting point.

Abou El Fadl, Khaled, with Tariq Ali, Milton Viorst, John Esposito, and others. *The Place of Tolerance in Islam.* Boston, 2002.

Abu-Nimer, Mohammed. *Nonviolence and Peace Building in Islam: Theory and Practice*. Gainesville, Fla., 2003.

*Ahmed, Leila. *A Border Passage: From Cairo to America—A Woman's Journey*. New York, 1999.

*———. *Women and Gender in Islam: Historical Roots of a Modern Debate*. New Haven and London, 1992.

*Ahmed, Salman, with Robert Schroeder. *Rock & Roll Jihad: A Muslim Rock Star's Revolution*. With an introduction by Melissa Etheridge. New York, 2010.

Al-Ali, Naji. *A Child in Palestine: The Cartoons of Naji al-Ali*. London and New York, 2009.

Al-Azmeh, Aziz. *Islam and Modernities*, 3rd ed. London and Brooklyn, N.Y., 2005.

Ansari, Zafar Ishaq, and John Esposito, eds. *Muslims and the West: Encounter and Dialogue*. Islamabad and Washington, D.C., 2001.

Appleby, R. Scott. *The Ambivalence of the Sacred: Religion, Violence, and Reconciliation*. Lanham, Md., Boulder, Colo., New York, and Oxford, 2000.

———, ed. *Spokesmen for the Despised: Fundamentalist Leaders of the Middle East*. Chicago and London, 1997.

Armstrong, Karen. *The Battle for God: A History of Fundamentalism*. London and New York, 2000.

*———. *Islam: A Short History*. London and New York, 2000.

———. *Jerusalem: One City, Three Faiths*. London and New York, 1996.

*Aslan, Reza. *How to Win a Cosmic War: God, Globalization, and the End of the War on Terror*. New York, 2009.

———. *No God But God: The Origins, Evolution, and Future of Islam*. London and New York, 2005.

Avineri, Shlomo. *The Making of Modern Zionism: The Intellectual Origins of the Jewish State*. London, 1981.

Avishai, Bernard. *The Tragedy of Zionism: Revolution and Democracy in the Land of Israel*. New York, 1985.

*Bauman, Zygmunt. *Modernity and the Holocaust*. Ithaca, N.Y., 1989.

Boone, Kathleen C. *The Bible Tells Them So: The Discourse of Protestant Fundamentalism*. London, 1990.

Choueiri, Youssef M. *Islamic Fundamentalism*. London, 1990.

Delong-Bas, Natana J., *Wahhabi Islam: From Revival and Reform to Global Jihad*. Oxford, 2004.

Djait, Hichem. *Europe and Islam: Cultures and Modernity.* Berkeley, 1985.

*Elon, Amos. *The Israelis: Fathers and Sons.* Rev. ed. London, 1984.

Esposito, John. *The Future of Islam.* New York and Oxford, 2010.

———. *Unholy War: Terror in the Name of Islam.* New York and Oxford, 2002.

———, ed. *Voices of Resurgent Islam.* New York and Oxford, 1983.

*Esposito, John, with Dahlia Mogahed. *Who Speaks for Islam? What a Billion Muslims Really Think, Based on the World's Gallup Poll.* New York, 2007.

Fischer, Michael J. *Iran: From Religious Dispute to Revolution.* Cambridge, Mass., and London, 1980.

Fisk, Robert. *Pity the Nation: Lebanon at War.* London, 1990.

Friedman, Robert J. *Zealots for Zion: Inside Israel's West Bank Settlement Movement.* New York, 1992.

Gole, Nilufa. *The Forbidden Modern: Civilization and Veiling.* Ann Arbor, Mich., 1996.

Gopin, Marc. *Between Eden and Armageddon: The Future of World Religions, Violence, and Peacemaking.* Oxford and New York, 2000.

*———. *Holy War, Holy Peace: How Religion Can Bring Peace to the Middle East.* New York and Oxford, 2002.

Gorenberg, Gershom. *The Accidental Empire: Israel and the Birth of the Settlements, 1967–1977.* New York, 2006.

Heikal, Mohamed. *Autumn of Fury: The Assassination of Sadat.* London, 1984.

Hertzberg, Arthur. *The Zionist Idea.* New York, 1969.

Hilterman, Joost R. *A Poisonous Affair: America, Iraq, and the Gassing of Halabja.* Cambridge, U.K., 2007.

*Holmes, Jonathan. *Fallujah: Eyewitness Testimony from Iraq's Besieged City.* London, 2007.

Hourani, Albert. *Islam in European Thought.* Cambridge, U.K., 1991.

Hroub, Khaled. *Hamas: Political Thought and Practice.* Washington, D.C., 2000.

*Karmi, Ghada. *In Search of Fatima: A Palestinian Story.* London and New York, 2002.

———. *Married to Another Man: Israel's Dilemma in Palestine.* London and Ann Arbor, 2007.

Keddie, Nikki R. *Roots of Revolution: An Interpretive History of Modern Iran.* New Haven and London, 1981.

————. *Scholars, Saints and Sufis: Muslim Religious Institutions in the Middle East Since 1500.* Berkeley, Los Angeles, and London, 1972.

————, ed. *Religion and Politics in Iran: Shiism from Quietism to Revolution.* New Haven and London, 1983.

Kepel, Gilles. *The Prophet and Pharaoh: Muslim Extremism in Egypt.* Trans. Jon Rothschild. London, 1985.

*Keshavarz, Fatemeh. *Jasmine and Stars: Reading More Than Lolita in Tehran.* Chapel Hill, N.C., 2007.

*Klausen, Jytte. *The Cartoons That Shook the World.* New Haven and London, 2009. One of the best analyses of the Danish cartoon crisis.

Klein, Menachem. *Jerusalem: The Contested City.* London, 1988.

Kurzman, Charles, ed. *Liberal Islam: A Sourcebook.* New York and Oxford, 1998.

Lawrence, Bruce B. *Defenders of God: The Fundamentalist Revolt Against the Modern Age.* London and New York, 1990.

Lincoln, Bruce. *Holy Terrors: Thinking About Religion After September 11.* 2nd ed. Chicago and London, 2003.

Lumbard, Joseph E. B., ed. *Islam, Fundamentalism, and the Betrayal of Tradition: Essays by Western Muslim Scholars.* With a foreword by Seyyed Hoseein Nasr. Bloomington, Ind., 2004.

Lustick, Ian S. *For the Land and the Lord: Jewish Fundamentalism in Israel.* New York, 1988.

Malik, Kenan. *From Fatwa to Jihad: The Rushdie Affair and Its Legacy.* London, 2009.

Mastnak, Tomaz. *Crusading Peace: Christendom, the Muslim World, and Western Political Order.* Berkeley and Los Angeles, 2002.

*Mernissi, Fatima. *Women in Islam: An Historical and Theological Inquiry.* Trans. Mary Jo Lakeland. Oxford, 1991.

Milton-Edwards, Beverley. *Islamic Politics in Palestine.* London and New York, 1996.

*Mohsin, Hamid. *The Reluctant Fundamentalist.* London, 2007. A beautifully written novel and an international best seller that gives nuanced insight into the world seen from Pakistan.

Momen, Moojan. *An Introduction to Shii Islam.* New Haven and London, 1985.

**Mottahedeh, Roy. *The Mantle of the Prophet: Religion and Politics in Iran.* London, 1985. This gets two stars, because it is a perfect introduction to the spirituality, history, and culture of Iran, which follows the life story of a young ayatollah and his friends in the decades before the Islamic Revolution.

Muzaffar, Chandra. *Global Ethic or Global Hegemony? Reflections on Religion, Human Dignity and Civilisational Interaction.* London, 2005.

———. *Muslims, Dialogue, Terror.* Selangore, Malaysia, 2003.

Nasr, Vali. *Islamic Leviathan: Islam and the Making of State Power.* Oxford and New York, 2001.

*———. *The Shia Revival: How Conflicts Within Islam Will Shape the Future.* New York, 2005.

———. *The Vanguard of the Islamic Revolution: The Jama'at-Islami of Pakistan.* London and New York, 1994.

Noll, Mark A., ed. *Religion and American Politics: From the Colonial Period to the 1980s.* Oxford and New York, 1990.

*Oz, Amos. *In the Land of Israel.* Trans. Maurice Goldberg-Bartura. London, 1983.

———. *My Michael.* Trans. Nicholas de Lange. London, 1972.

Ramadan, Tariq. *Radical Reform: Islamic Ethics and Liberation.* Oxford, 2009.

———. *Western Muslims and the Future of Islam.* Oxford, 2004.

*———. *What I Believe.* Oxford and New York, 2010.

Ravitsky, Aviezer. *Messianism, Zionism, and Jewish Religious Radicalism.* Trans. Michael Swirsky and Jonathan Chipman. Chicago and London, 1993.

Rodinson, Maxime. *Europe and the Mystique of Islam.* Trans. Roger Veinus. London, 1988.

*Rogan, Eugene. *The Arabs: A History.* London, 2009.

Roy, Olivier. *Globalized Islam: The Search for a New Ummah.* New York, 2004.

Sachedina, Abdulaziz. *The Islamic Roots of Democratic Pluralism.* New York and Oxford, 2001.

Said, Edward. *Orientalism: Western Conceptions of Orient.* New York, 1978.

Sajoo, Amyn B. *Civil Society in the Muslim World: Contemporary Perspectives.* London and New York, 2002.

*Schechter, Jack. *The Land of Israel: Its Theological Dimensions; A Study of a Promise and of a Land's "Holiness."* Lanham, Md., 2010.

*Schweid, Eliezer. *The Land of Israel: National Home or Land of Destiny.* Trans. Deborah Greniman. London and Toronto, 1985.

Sick, Gary. *All Fall Down: America's Fateful Encounter with Iran*. London, 1985.

Silberstein, Lawrence. *Jewish Fundamentalism in Comparative Perspective: Religion, Ideology, and the Crisis of Modernity*. New York and London, 1993.

Soroush, Abdolkarim. *Reason, Freedom, and Democracy in Islam: Essential Writings of Abdolkarim Soroush*. Trans. and ed. Mahmoud Sadri and Ahmad Sadri. New York and Oxford, 2000.

Sprinzak, Ehud. *The Ascendance of Israel's Radical Right*. Oxford and New York, 1991.

*Takeh, Ray. *Guardians of the Revolution: Iran and the World in the Age of the Ayatollahs*. New York and Oxford, 2009.

*Tarnas, Richard. *The Passion of the Western Mind: Understanding the Ideas That Have Shaped Our World View*. New York and London, 1991.

Tibi, Bassam. *The Crisis of Political Islam: A Pre-Industrial Culture in the Scientific-Technological Age*. Salt Lake City, Utah, 1988.

Wolfe, Michael. *Hadj: A Pilgrimage to Mecca*. London, 1993.

———, ed., with the producers of Beliefnet. *Taking Back Islam: American Muslims Reclaim Their Faith*. Emmaus, Pa., 2002.

Yovel, Yirmanyahu. *Dark Riddle: Hegel, Nietzsche, and the Jews*. Cambridge, U.K., 1998.

Zaru, Jean. *Occupied with Nonviolence: A Palestinian Woman Speaks Out*. Minneapolis, 2008.

A NOTE ABOUT THE AUTHOR

Karen Armstrong is the author of numerous other books on religious affairs, including *The Case for God, A History of God, The Battle for God, Holy War, Islam, Buddha,* and *The Great Transformation,* and a memoir, *The Spiral Staircase.* In February 2008 she was awarded the TED Prize and began working with TED on the Charter for Compassion, created online by the general public; crafted by leading thinkers in Judaism, Christianity, Islam, Hinduism, Buddhism, and Confucianism; and launched globally in fall 2009. She lives in London.

A NOTE ON THE TYPE

This book was set in Chaparral, an Adobe original typeface designed by Carol Twombly and released in 1997. The
inspiration for Chaparral was a page of lettering from
a sixteenth-century manuscript, adapted by Twombly
into a readable slab serif design. Unlike geometric slab
serif fonts, Chaparral has varying letter proportions that
give it an accessible and friendly appearance. Chaparral
was the last typeface Twombly designed before she left
Adobe and perhaps retired from type design in 1999.

Composed by Creative Graphics, Allentown, Pennsylvania

Printed and bound by RR Donnelley, Harrisonburg, Virginia

Designed by Maggie Hinders